Techniques
for
Police Instructors

Fourth Printing

Techniques

for

Police Instructors

By

JOHN C. KLOTTER

Professor, Police Administration
Associate Director
Southern Police Institute
University of Louisville
Louisville, Kentucky
Formerly
Special Agent, Federal Bureau of Investigation
and
Director, Kentucky Division of Probation and Parole

CHARLES C THOMAS · PUBLISHER
Springfield · Illinois · U.S.A.

Published and Distributed Throughout the World by
CHARLES C THOMAS • PUBLISHER
Bannerstone House
301-327 East Lawrence Avenue, Springfield, Illinois, U.S.A.

© *1963, by* CHARLES C THOMAS • PUBLISHER
ISBN 0-398-01029-3
Library of Congress Catalog Card Number: 63-11526

First Printing, 1963
Second Printing, 1971
Third Printing, 1974
Fourth Printing, 1978

With THOMAS BOOKS *careful attention is given to all details of
manufacturing and design. It is the Publisher's desire to present books that
are satisfactory as to their physical qualities and artistic possibilities and
appropriate for their particular use.* THOMAS BOOKS *will be true to those
laws of quality that assure a good name and good will.*

Printed in the United States of America
R-1

PREFACE

Efficiency in police operations requires well qualified and well trained personnel. In the police service, most of the training must be accomplished within the department. Without training, even the most carefully chosen person will not be qualified to perform the many and varied tasks required of the law enforcement officer.

In preparing this book, the author has taken a practical approach to training. No effort has been made to discuss psychological aspects of learning or detailed theories as are usually included in books designed for students majoring in education. The material is specific and is designed to give the full-time police instructor as well as the instructor who teaches only occasionally some effective tools in teaching.

To emphasize the suggested method of preparing and presenting the lesson, each chapter is presented in three parts. The "introduction" states the reasons the chapter is included, the objectives to be accomplished and the procedure to be followed. In the "body" the teaching points are presented and discussed in detail. The "closing" in each chapter briefly reviews the points presented and ends with a statement emphasizing the importance of remembering the material presented.

Often the experienced police officer has important knowledge gained through study and experience. This book is designed to enable the officer to communicate the information to others.

J. C. K.

CONTENTS

Techniques
for
Police Instructors

Chapter 1

FOUNDATIONS FOR LEARNING
INTRODUCTION

Reasons for Chapter

At no time in the history of policing has there been greater need for the officer to pass on what he has learned to others. The police activity has become more and more specialized and trained men are necessary to effectively carry out the duties of the police agency. In order for the police instructor to teach the student he must not only know the subject matter thoroughly but be completely familiar with the fundamental elements necessary in any instructional situation.

Objectives of the Chapter

In this chapter each element of the four fundamental elements in the instructional situation will be discussed. The reader will be able to obtain an understanding of the overall foundation on which all learning is predicated.

Review

This is the first chapter in this book. Before reading this chapter the reader should read the preface thoroughly for an understanding of the procedure followed and the overall purpose of the book.

Procedure

This chapter is divided into four parts. Each of the four foundations in the instructional situation will be further divided, discussed, and summarized.

BODY

The foundation supports the structure. The parts of the foundation which support the learning structure are the student, the instructor, the development process, and the learning climate. We shall discuss each of these.

The Student

The instructor must understand that each student is different. He must see the course of instruction from the point of view of the LEARNER and plan accordingly.

a. Characteristics common to most police students. Each student is, of course, different in some ways and the instructor must consider these differences, but there are some characteristics which are common to most police students. These characteristics will vary from class to class and the instructor must evaluate each class. For example, the characteristics common to a recruit class will not be the same as those common to an inservice training class or to a class receiving specialized training.

Some of the characteristics common to police students are as follows.

(1) Most of the students are mentally, emotionally, and physically mature. With the selection procedures now applied in most police departments, men who are not mature are generally eliminated. The police instructor can, as a rule, plan his instruction for mature men.

(2) Most men have a serious purpose. The instructor must keep in mind that it is his responsibility to motivate the students, but he can also assume that most police officers are anxious to learn and get the most from their training. Some methods of motivating students will be covered in the following chapters.

(3) Students are interested in the WHY and HOW of what they are taught. A student will usually judge instruction in terms of why he should learn this and how he can apply this knowledge. They are keenly interested in a practical application of theory and knowledge.

Too often the student can not see how some subjects will be of benefit to him. Too often the student can see only the immediate application and can not project himself into the future. One of the most difficult tasks of the instructor is to explain the "why" of the subject. This, however, must be accomplished or the student will be in class only in body.

(4) Students respect instructors who know the subject mat-

ter and have the ability to effectively present the subject matter. Not only do students respect good instructors, they are quick to detect the incompetent.

(5) Men attending police classes are capable of mastering the essentials of the police training. The men who are selected for policing in our modern police agencies have the mental capacity to master the material presented. If not, they should be eliminated. The instructor must determine the characteristics and background of each class but can usually be satisfied that with proper motivation and teaching methods the student can learn the material.

The instructor who recognizes these and other common characteristics of the students and carefully studies each class to determine the background of the class, will have a starting point on which to build further learning.

b. Fundamental principles to be followed by the instructor in his contact with the student.

The instructor must remember that the student, especially in the police field, is mature and not easily fooled. The student is quick to recognize the instructor who is qualified but just as quick to recognize the instructor who is trying to bluff or cover up his lack of knowledge. The instructor who succeeds must remember that certain principles must be followed when he has contact with the student.

Be Patient

One of the first habits that must be developed by the instructor is patience. If it appears that the student is slow in grasping material presented, the instructor should first ask himself, "Have I failed to teach?" It is often difficult for the instructor to understand why the student is not learning as rapidly as the instructor thinks he should. If this occurs, the instructor should re-evaluate the background of the student, check the motivation methods he has used, and reconsider the level of the material presented. He should never lose patience.

Admit the Fact that Answers are Not Known and Find the Answer

The instructor should never bluff to cover up lack of knowledge. The instructor should know the subject matter thoroughly. Even the experienced instructor will be asked questions he can not answer at that time. If he does not know the answer, he should admit the fact that he does not know, advise the class that he does not know, but that he will look up the answer and give it to the class later.

Students will soon lose respect for the instructor who tries to bluff to cover up lack of knowledge.

Use Words and Phrases That the Student Understands

There is a place for technical words and many syllabled words. The instructor must remember, however, that he is trying to teach the student, not to impress the student with his vocabulary. Again it is necessary for the instructor to know the background of the students in order to determine his choice of words. If in doubt, the instructor should use words he knows the student will understand. His job is to present ideas. He should choose the words which best convey these ideas to the particular group he is teaching.

Don't Use Profanity or Obscenity

The instructor who continuously uses profanity not only shows he has a limited vocabulary but soon loses dignity and the respect of the class. It is often tempting to use profane or obscene language to impress the class. The good instructor does not have to resort to these methods. There is usually at least one person in the class who takes offense at this with the result that the instructor loses the attention of that person. Profanity is the language of frustration.

Don't Use Sarcasm or Ridicule

The resentful student will not have his mind on learning. The instructor is in a place of authority when he is teaching a class. Students are in no position to retort. When sarcasm or ridicule is used by the instructor, the student is resentful. Not only will the person ridiculed be resentful but the other students will be offended because a fellow student is so badly treated. There can be no rapport between the class and the instructor who ridicules the class.

Don't Talk Down to a Class

Make the class feel that you consider yourself fortunate to have the privilege of sharing with them the knowledge you have acquired. Too often an instructor loses the class completely because he gives the impression he is much above the class. This does not mean that the instructor will not keep control of the class. The instructor can maintain discipline without "talking down."

The Instructor

The second foundation for learning is the instructor. There must be someone to give information as well as someone to receive it.

Qualifications of the Instructor

There are certain qualifications which the instructor must possess if he is to do an effective job of teaching.

(1) *Knowledge of the Subject.*

The instructional situation breaks down if there is any doubt concerning the instructor's knowledge of the subject. If the instructor doesn't know the subject matter, how can he teach others? Yet too often the instructor attempts to teach material knowing that he is not thoroughly prepared.

As far as possible, the instructor should have both field experience and a thorough knowledge of the training literature. The instructor makes a serious mistake, however, if he assumes that his field experience alone gives him sufficient knowledge to teach without further planning and preparation. The experience he has had should enable him to evaluate the available written material and make the instruction more realistic to the student.

The instructor should not only be familiar with the material he will actually present but material which is related to the subject. He must know more than he will ever have time to teach and be prepared to answer any question relative to the subject which might be asked.

(2) *Knowledge of Methods of Instruction.*

Knowing the subject is not enough. The knowledge must be conveyed to the student. Many skilled men do poorly as instructors because they do not know how to present the subject matter. Every person who is to instruct should first be trained in the methods of instruction. The officer who has knowledge of the methods of instruction will be much more effective in his instruction. More instructors fail because they do not know how to instruct than because they are not familiar with the subject matter.

(3) *Leadership Ability.*

Classes must be managed before they can be taught. In order for the class to run smoothly, the instructor must display the qualities of leadership. The instructor must keep the class under control. The officer in the police service who fails to display leadership in the classroom soon loses the class and no learning takes place.

The instructor also must not forget that he, by his leadership actions, is setting the example for the students.

(4) *Professional Attitude.*

The instructor must have the proper attitude toward his students, his subject, and the training program. His attitude will have a tremendous influence on students' attitudes and morale. Students tend to adopt both the attitude of the instructor and his point of view toward the subject and training. We have all seen instructors meander into the classroom, slouch down in the chair and begin the instruction by saying, "Well, this subject has been assigned to me and I have to teach it. Let's get this hour over with." Obviously, the attitude of the student will reflect the attitude of the instructor and very little will be accomplished. Compare this with the instructor who is well prepared, enters the classroom ready and eager to teach.

The attitude of the instructor should be friendly but professional. Attitudes often have a greater total effect upon the students' future success than do the skills and the information learned.

(5) *Sincerity.*

The insincere instructor causes the student to lose confidence and interest. Attitudes of the student are determined by the attitudes of the instructor. Many instructors who lack some of the other qualifications are successful in developing ideas in the student because they are sincere.

(6) *Enthusiasm.*

The enthusiasm of the instructor is catching. Lack of enthusiasm will cause even the best planned lesson to fail in its objective.

(7) *Salesmanship.*

Closely related to enthusiasm is salesmanship. After all, teaching is selling the material to the student. As in other types of legitimate selling the salesman must first believe in his subject. He must be thoroughly familiar with his product and enthusiastically sell it to the students.

These are some of the qualifications of the instructor. Other obvious requirements are a sense of humor, pleasing personal appearance, and the desire to do a good job.

Development of the Instructor

Instructors are made, not born. Some might not agree with this statement but certainly no one would argue that a person is born with all of the complex skills that are required in teaching. It is true that the person must have the mental capacity to learn to be an instructor. But this is only one factor in becoming a competent instructor. Men become good instructors primarily through study and hard work. How successful the instructor is depends upon his desire to develop his abilities to the maximum degree. No instructor is ever perfect. The fact that the instructor has taught for many years does not mean that he has made significant improvement. The question arises, "How can the instructor improve or how can he develop as an instructor?" Listed below are some of the methods or techniques the instructor can use in improving his instructive qualities.

(1) Recognize that he can develop into a qualified instructor. Probably the most important step is for the person to recognize that qualities of the instructor can be developed. The proper mental attitude is the first step in becoming a qualified instructor. The instructor who says "I'm just not a born instructor" will, of course, never become an instructor. Anyone with the mental

capacity to learn instructional techniques can become a good instructor.

(2) Know what makes good instruction. It is, of course, impossible to improve as instructors if we do not know what the standards are. The instructor must start with an appreciation of the basic elements of his instruction. Some of the characteristics of the good instructor were listed under the previous heading. Others will be mentioned in later chapters in this book.

(3) Observe other instructors. Many ideas and techniques for presenting material can be acquired by watching other instructors. The instructor in attempting to improve his own instruction should observe those techniques used by the other instructor that are effective in presenting material. The instructor must be careful, however, that he does not imitate the other instructor. Few instructors capitalize on their own native abilities to the full extent but copy other instructors. The instructor should determine what other instructors do well and then develop his own techniques based on his outstanding abilities rather than on the abilities he admires but lacks. To a great extent two highly competent instructors can have radically different personalities and use entirely different techniques and both still be able to do a superior job of teaching.

(4) Analyze own Characteristics. The instructor in attempting to improve his instruction should analyze his own characteristics. If the instructor is honest with himself he will be able to determine which characteristics need improving. He should not only, however, determine his weaknesses as far as instruction is concerned but determine the strong points that he has as an instructor. Where he finds he has strong points the instructor should dwell on these points and correct the weakness as far as possible.

(5) Obtain evaluation by other instructors. Although self-criticism is probably the best means of becoming a better instructor it is often impossible for an instructor to evaluate his own work objectively. He should therefore actively seek the evaluation of other instructors, supervisors, and students. In doing this both the instructor who is seeking to improve and the instructors who are constructively criticising should have the proper attitude. He should evaluate the suggestions made by other instructors and accept them if they are legitimate.

(6) Concentrate on specific elements. A general attitude on the part of the instructor to do better while very commendable, rarely brings the significant improvement desired. Progress is made by concentrating upon specific techniques and working out a systematic plan for improvement. A self-analysis and an analysis by others is of no value if the instructor fails to improve his own instruction characteristics. If, for example, the instructor through analysis finds that one of his weak characteristics is knowledge of the subject matter being taught, he should, of course, take steps to improve this knowledge.

These steps will help the instructor to develop. It should be emphasized that this development is a continuous process. When one characteristic has been developed as far as possible then other characteristics should be worked on. Training is as complex as the students who are being trained. The good instructor is always alert to better methods and techniques of presenting material to the students.

The Development Process

We have indicated that two of the foundations for learning are the *student* and the *instructor*. Of course, no learning will take place unless something is done. By some means the knowledge and skills of the instructor must be conveyed to the student. Too often the instructor merely starts talking without having made plans, with no organized method of presenting the material, and with no plans to determine if the student has learned the material. Many educators have developed plans to be followed in preparing and presenting instruction. Under this heading we shall discuss one of the guides the instructor can use in planning and conducting his instruction. This guide is flexible and logical.

If the instructor follows the stages of instruction as listed and discussed, his instruction will be planned in an organized way, presented effectively and student learning will be evaluated. Each of these stages of discussion will be discussed thoroughly at a later period. However, here we shall discuss each of them as they relate to the entire instructional process.

Preparation

This is also known as the planning stage of instruction. In any phase of police work, action must be preceded by a plan.

Before the instructor can actually present the material to the student, he must plan his approach. In developing the student the instructor must analyze the specific procedures, skills, and information which are to be taught in this particular lesson and in the over-all course. He must organize the material so that the basic ideas are adapted to the student's background and needs. He must proceed from the simple to the complex and from the known to the unknown. In the preparation stage of instruction the instructor must consider not only the information to be taught but the time element, the background of the student, the degree of learning desired, and methods he can use in presenting the material. In this preparation stage the instructor must remember that mastery of the subject matter is only the first step of the instructional preparation.

The instructor must determine how to rouse the students' desire to learn and how to present the subject matter so that each member of the class learns all of the essential procedures and ideas. By review of the procedures to be followed and rehearsal, the instructor will be able to insure maximum student learning in a minimum amount of time. Also in the preparation or planning stage of instruction the instructor must determine the type of instruction he will use in teaching this particular lesson, the type of aids he will use in presenting the material to the students and formalize the instruction by preparing a complete lesson plan.

Presentation

The second stage of instruction is the presentation stage. In the presentation stage of instruction the actual teaching begins. If the preparation stage has been completed diligently, the presentation stage of instruction will be much easier. It is this stage of instruction that the instructor has been looking forward to in his preparation. Here is where the student actually gains knowledge and develops attitudes and appreciations.

The presentation stage of instruction is normally divided into three parts. It should be emphasized that these three parts will not necessarily be included in every instructional period. However, these three phases in the presentation stage, if considered properly, will help the instructor in organizing his material.

(1) *Introduction.*

In the introduction the students are prepared to receive the ideas which will be made available to them. In the introduction the instructor must obtain the attention of the students and make sure that the students are, "tuned in to the right station." Some of the best methods of obtaining the attention of the student will be discussed in a future chapter. Generally, in the introduction, the student is told what he is to learn, why he is to learn this particular material and the procedure to be followed in presenting the material.

(2) *Body.*

It is actually not until the second part of the presentation stage of instruction that the student is presented the material. Here the instructor makes new material available to the students by a variety of methods and procedures. The instructor not only helps the student obtain knowledge but guides the student in developing skills and attitudes.

In this stage of instruction the instructor not only tells the student but often shows the student how to perform a particular act. Depending upon the subject matter the instructor may use the lecture method, conference method, demonstration method, or a combination of all of these methods.

(3) *Closing.*

The third part of the presentation stage of instruction is the closing phase. In the introduction the student has been prepared for the material to be presented. In the body he has been presented with the material and the material has been made clear to him. In the closing the instructor should review the material, clear up any questions that may not have been answered or that are not clear to the student, and close with a statement that will make the student feel that he has accomplished something in the period or periods.

Application

The third stage of instruction is the application stage. This is called the "Doing" stage of instruction and is the stage where the student has an opportunity to apply the principles and procedures learned in the presentation stage of instruction. It should be pointed out again that it is not possible in every type of subject matter to use the application stage of instruction. At least not at the time the material has been presented. However, use of the application method, or application stage of instruction, will often give the students an opportunity to learn by doing. He will therefore remember the material longer and be able to use it better in the future. A future chapter will discuss some of the problems that must be met in this stage of instruction and some suggested procedures to be followed in this stage of instruction.

Evaluation

The instructor cannot be certain that the student has mastered the essentials unless some check is made. In some way the instructor must evaluate the learning of the student. Many techniques can be used to evaluate or to examine the degree of learning of the student. This evaluation stage of examination stage, if applied properly, is an important step in the learning process.

Critique

The final stage of instruction is the critique. Regardless of the type of evaluation used, a critique should follow to determine in which areas the students failed to learn. This stage of instruction completes the picture by clarifying any phases of instruction which are not completely understood. The critique should also follow an application phase of instruction. That is, the instructor should point out to the student in which areas he has performed satisfactorily and in which areas he needs improvement.

Again it is emphasized that the five stages of instruction discussed here will not apply in every situation. It is also emphasized that the instructor will often be using several of the stages of instruction at one time. For example, the instructor could present the material orally; apply the application stage by letting the students do the thing that the instructor has told them to do; use the evaluation stage by giving a short examination to determine if the material has been used properly; and conduct a critique immediately after the application to determine if the skill being taught has been performed properly.

The stages of instruction are not intended to cause instruction to become artificial or stereotyped. However, the instructor, if he considers these stages of instruction in his planning, will be more likely to cover the material properly and develop more complete learning.

The Learning Climate

In discussing the foundations for learning it is necessary to mention the learning climate. One writer said that a good school consists of a qualified instructor on one end of a log and a receptive student on the other end. There is much truth in this. However, studies have shown that the student learns more where the climate for learning is good. Certainly the physical environment to a great extent determines how efficiently the student will learn. No matter how good the instructor is or how interesting his presentation may be, the student will have difficulty paying attention if he is not comfortable. If the student is unable to pay attention due to the physical conditions, it is very unlikely that he will learn very much. Thirty minutes of undivided attention is worth more than two hours of half attention and half interest.

A check list that the instructor can follow in making sure that the learning climate is the best is as follows:

a. *Be concerned with the comfort of the students.* The instructor should put himself in the place of the students and determine if their physical comfort is as good as possible under conditions present. He should make sure that the temperature in the room is not too hot or not too cold, that the light is not glaring in the eyes of the student, and that the light is sufficient for the student to see properly. He should see that there are sufficient chairs for the students and that chairs are of the type on which the student can write. He should make sure that the seating arrangement is such that all the students can see and hear the instructor and the training aids if training aids are used. He should be sure that distracting noises and movements are eliminated or minimized. He must also make sure that the area is clean.

b. *Check classroom equipment and aids.* The instructor can create a better climate for learning if he determines in advance that all the equipment he will need and all the training aids he will need are on hand and in good shape. He should remove all distracting materials from the walls and keep training aids out of sight until time for them to be used. An aid lying around the room will distract the students from the particular material being presented at the time.

c. *Introduce the instructor properly*. The learning climate is made better if the instructor introduces himself or if someone else introduces the instructor. The rapport between the student and the instructor is increased by this introduction. The student likes to know something about the person who is instructing. To a great extent the material presented will be influenced by the background of the instructor. Therefore the student is in a better position to interpret the material presented if he knows this background.

d. *Designate topic*. It is a good practice to have a card prepared designating the topic which will be discussed or to write this topic upon the blackboard. This leaves the student with no doubt as to what the topic of discussion is. Often an instructor will start teaching without designating the topic and the student will spend some minutes trying to get on the same "frequency" as the instructor. Of course this is a loss of time and is unnecessary.

CLOSING

Summary

In this chapter we have discussed the foundations of learning. Under this heading we have discussed, 1. The Student, 2. The Instructor, 3. The Development Process, and 4. The Learning Climate. These four parts of the foundation are necessary before learning can take place. The instructor who carefully considers these foundations will be able to build a better student.

Closing Statement

The instructor must remember when preparing and presenting his lesson that his job is to not only teach the subject matter but to teach the student.

Chapter 2

THE LEARNING PROCESS
INTRODUCTION

Reasons for Chapter

Before the instructor can effectively teach he must understand the learning process. The instructor who does not consider the student, the way he learns, and the principles of learning, wastes the time of the student as well as his own time. On the other hand, the instructor who has an understanding of the processes by which the student learns will not be limited in his instruction to the methods used by others. He can devise his own procedures to meet the special needs of the training situation; he can use variety in his instruction; can use his own instructor qualities to the best advantage; and can develop understanding on the part of the student.

Objective of Chapter

The purpose of this chapter is to discuss the types of learning and the principles with which the instructor must be familiar to insure learning on the part of the student.

Review of Previous Instruction

In the preceding chapter we discussed the foundations for learning; those foundations on which learning is built. In this chapter we discuss the processes that are followed in building on this foundation.

Procedure

The material to be discussed in this chapter will be discussed in the following order; a. Definitions of learning and instruction, b. Channels of learning, c. Types of learning, and d. Principles of learning.

BODY

Learning Defined

Many educators have attempted to define learning. Some of

17

these definitions are too complicated to have meaning. Others are not broad enough in their scope. One writer defines learning as an intelligent adaptation to changing conditions. Another authority defines learning as the process of acquiring knowledge. We will learn that this is too limited as learning includes more than the acquiring of mere knowledge. Perhaps the best definition, especially as far as police officers are concerned, is the definition which puts emphasis on the student's ability to perform as the result of learning. This definition is as follows: "Learning is defined as the process of acquiring new knowledge, skills, techniques, and appreciations which will enable the individual to do something that he could not do before."

Under this definition if the student is no better equipped to do something at the end of a lesson, or training period, there has been no learning. Learning is not a passive absorption of knowledge but is essentially an active process. This definition at first glance appears to be a very restricted definition of learning. However, it is hard to dream up any situation where the acquiring of a new skill, new knowledge, new techniques or new appreciations will not enable the individual to do something that he could not do before or do it better. All new knowledge will to some extent affect the over-all thinking of an individual.

Instruction Defined

Instruction is more than standing or sitting before a class and stating or presenting ideas. When we defined learning we emphasized that learning was an active process and not just a passive absorption of knowledge. Instruction then is best defined as, "All of the instructor activities that contribute toward leading, guiding, directing and controlling the thoughts and actions of the students as they learn." Here emphasis is placed upon learning by the student. The question is then presented, is there any instruction if there is no learning? If we apply the definition we have just given there is, of course, no instruction if no learning results. Instruction, in short, is everything the instructor does that helps the student to learn. This would include what he says, what he does, training aids he uses, and all other activities which help the student to learn. If the instructor will keep this in mind, he will be a better instructor. We can say then that if the *stu-*

dent doesn't learn the instructor doesn't teach. This can be compared to the theory of sound. That is: there is no sound if there is no one there to hear the sound. Vibrations are in the air but the sound does not take place until someone's ear is there to transfer these vibrations into sound.

Channels of Learning

All ideas from whatever origin reach the mind through one or more of the five physical senses. They reach the mind through the senses of *sight, hearing, touch, taste, smell* or a combination of several of these. Through these senses the individual makes contact with the things about him. As the result of these contacts through the senses he makes certain responses which lead to the learning of new knowledge, the improving of certain habits or the changing of his attitude or points of view. The instructor should think of these various senses as five circuits which reach the brain and consider the concept that the more circuits that can be brought into use the greater will be the chances of learning. If two circuits can be used to reach the brain, rather than one, more learning will take place by the student. The instructor should, therefore, rather than just tell the student, show the student, if practicable, and also let the student do the act himself. If the subject matter is of such a nature that the senses of taste and smell would increase his chances of learning, then these should be used also.

The instructor is concerned with getting ideas to the mind of the student and making them register there. It is important to note that *not* all of the impressions picked up by the senses reach the mind. The student might hear the spoken word of the instructor or see the charts used by the instructor, but if the instruction is not registered, assimilated and retained there is no learning. There is a great deal of truth in the old saying that some instruction goes in one ear and out the other.

Types of Learning

In considering the learning process it is helpful for the instructor to discuss the types of learning. Although the instructor must keep in mind that he is teaching the individual as well as the subject matter and the types of learning are not separate and distinct, he can plan his instruction more effectively if he considers the types of learning. The instructor must keep in mind that some lessons will include one or more types of learning and he should not always try to fit the material he is to present exclusively into one of these types.

Knowledge

Knowledge can be defined as a type of learning where the student is helped to understand and retain facts, procedures, principles, and information. For example: the police officer in a recruit school must learn the laws and ordinances under which he will operate. In addition, he must also know the principles of firing a weapon upon which he will develop skills, techniques and appreciations. If the primary objective of the instructor is to teach knowledge, the approach, of course, will de different than it would be if the primary purpose were to teach skills.

Skills

Skill can be defined as the act or a series of acts which are performed instinctively without the conscious effort of thinking. If the instructor's purpose in a particular class or a group of classes is to teach a skill, he will approach the training differently than he would if he were teaching a knowledge subject. Skills are not truly learned until they become almost instinctive. Of course, they will not become instinctive unless there is much practice. Therefore, the instructor in planning his lesson where skills are involved must give much more time to practice. Some examples of skills that are taught in police training are: driving the vehicles, operating weapons, and self defense.

Techniques

Techniques are a way of thinking and acting based upon knowledge and often upon skills as well. Often techniques must be studied in the classroom first but they must be practiced before they can be learned. Even though techniques are based upon knowledge or skill, they require attention and thought in their application. Even though the instruction in the classroom is the same, each individual will develop a different technique. The instructor, therefore, in preparing to teach a technique must take into consideration the fact that each student is different. Techniques are developed by applying knowledge and skills and cannot be developed adequately until there has been much practice. As an example, in policing, each officer will develop a technique of arrest, a technique of approaching a vehicle, a technique of teaching other students. Technique, then, is more than knowledge and more than a skill. It is the individual method of application.

Appreciations

No other type of learning has been so misunderstood and misapplied as appreciation. Appreciation can be the chief and ultimate aim of teaching. Appreciation cannot be taught in the same sense in which skills and facts are taught. However, a foundation can be furnished upon which appreciations may be developed. It is difficult to adequately define appreciations, however, it is usually defined in terms of attitudes, ideals, interests, habits, likes and dislikes. It is well recognized that the attitude of the student in applying skills, knowledge and techniques will to a great extent determine how effective his efforts will be. The other types of learning are of little value if the appreciation factor is missing. Unfortunately, attitudes and ideals of the police officer are often left to chance.

The instructional program should include periods for developing appreciations. This type of learning should also be kept in mind when the instructor is teaching skills, techniques and knowledge. It is very difficult to measure these qualities with any degree of objectivity and the standards by their very nature must be comparative ones. Still a careful observer can, over a period of time, determine the ideals and attitudes of the police officer by how effectively he applies the other types of learning.

Principles of Learning

Before the pilot is authorized to fly his plane he must learn and understand the principles of flight. He must understand the principle of lift, the principle of thrust and the other principles which give him an understanding of flight. In the same way, the instructor must know the general principles of learning before he can teach properly. These principles are generalizations of rules which, if properly applied by the instructor will make learning more efficient. Other principles could be added and these to some extent are overlapping. The most important principles, however, that the instructor must keep in mind concerning learning are as follows:

Motivation

The student must be motivated to learn. Since learning is an active process the student must be motivated to learn for himself. The instructor must, therefore, create a desire to learn. This desire must come from within the student. It is often necessary for the instructor to properly motivate students, especially as to the particular subject matter being taught. One might argue that it is not necessary to motivate police officers since they have all been carefully selected. They should have the desire within themselves to learn. Unfortunately, however, this is not the case in all instances. It is often necessary for the instructor to motivate the student before the student will learn. This is especially true in some subjects where the police officer does not see the practical need for the subject immediately. Some of the techniques which may be employed by the instructor to secure motivation will be covered under the next heading.

Purpose

Learning is much more rapid and effective when it is purposeful. An individual rapidly acquires skills, knowledge, techniques and appreciation when these achievements are necessary in order to attain the realization of some purpose. The more intense the purpose of the individual the more rapid the learning. The instructor should try to create situations in which the need for acquisition of knowledge and skill will be obvious. The instructor should emphasize the objective of the particular lesson by making frequent references to the purpose as he covers the main points of the unit. Also, the purpose or the objective of the whole subject should be made clear and how this fits into the over-all needs of the student. Stating the purpose in terms of the exact procedures and information required for use in the field gives the student a purpose for learning this subject.

Adjustment

The instructor should keep in mind that when the student learns either skills, knowledge or techniques he to a certain extent must make mental adjustments. The new knowledge that he has gained may give him more facts upon which to form new attitudes and opinions. To a certain extent the student has grown in his learning and necessarily some change will take place in his thinking. One instructor so aptly put this by saying, "I am a part of every student I teach." The growth and adjustment may not be immediately decernable but the adjustment is taking place.

Activity

The instructor should also remember that in learning skills and techniques and to some extent in gaining in knowledge and in developing attitudes there must be some activity on the part of the student. We often call this, "learning by doing," however, activity can be present without actually doing the thing being taught. For example: We don't often think of activity being used in teaching such things as law and ordinances. However, it can be much better understood by the student if problem type questions are asked the student, if practical exercises are given to the student, and by the use of the conference type method of instruction. If the instructor uses ingenuity and plans his lessons, this principle can be applied in almost any type of teaching.

It is very important that the instructor keep in mind that practice does not make perfect unless the practice is correct. If the practice is in error it would only serve to develop wrong concepts and habits. The primary considerations should be first that the student should be kept mentally and physically active; and secondly that the activity should be directed to a specific purpose.

Association

The student associates new material with past learning. Something new is learned by means of associating this with something the student already knows. Because of this the instructor must as much as possible know the students. He should also be very careful in presenting ideas so that the whole class will interpret the ideas properly. The subject matter should be explained by using illustrations and words which the student understands. If the instructor is not careful, one student who has a very different background from other students will interpret the instruction entirely differently from that intended by the instructor.

The instructor in police training can be more sure that his instruction is clear by giving illustrations drawn from past experiences of the student and relating these past experiences to the new material. The instructor can also check with the class to see if his material is being interpreted properly by asking oral questions. The instructor must recognize that his own past experiences are not necessarily the same as those of the students he is teaching. Often he might think a point is clear to the students because of his past experiences while to the student who has not had these experiences the instruction is not clear at all.

Realism

Closely associated with some of the other principles of learning we have discussed is the principle of realism. Learning is more effective when it is realistic. Realism involves two considerations. First, is the material presented realistic from the standpoint of application? Will the officer who is receiving the training have any use for this in the field? Another way of putting this is, is this material functional? Often it is necessary for the instructor, as indicated under the principle of purpose, to make clear to the class that the instruction is realistic as far as application is concerned.

The second aspect of realism asks this question. Is the subject matter realistic as far as the level of the class is concerned? If the instruction is over the heads of the men, and if they cannot associate it with past learning; it is unrealistic as far as that group of students is concerned. For example: it would be unrealistic to present the Einstein Theory of Relativity to a class of police recruits. This does not mean that the instructor cannot present difficult subject matter, but it does mean that the instructor must, in some situations, proceed less rapidly in order to make the material realistic to the student.

Incidental Learning

Incidental learning refers to the learning which occurs while the learner is doing something else. The instructor may be teaching scientific crime investigation but the student learns many things in addition to the skills and information being taught. Such things as habits, attitudes and character traits are learned almost exclusively through this process of incidental learning. In some instances these outcomes are more important or as important as the information and skills which are being taught. These habits, interest, attitudes and appreciation may be either favorable or unfavorable, depending upon the instructor. Too often the instructor fails to consider this phase of learning in his preparation. However, this is just as much responsibility of the instructor as the specific information being taught. The police instructor who has carefully planned his program will teach desirable attitudes to the students even though there is no specific subject which is directed at teaching attitudes.

Often the student develops the same attitude toward a subject as that exhibited by the instructor. Therefore, if the instructor takes a lackadasical attitude toward the instruction there is little chance that the student will consider it seriously. On the other hand, if the instructor demonstrates sincerity and enthusiasm the men will feel the same way toward the material being presented. There is no better way to develop appreciations than by example. The instructor must, therefore, remain alert to this fact and conduct his instruction accordingly.

When we consider that so much of our learning is through this process it is impossible to place too much stress on this principle of learning. The instructor teaches "the whole student, not just the subject matter."

We have discussed the most important principles of learning. The instructor, as indicated, must understand these principles before he can teach effectively and efficiently. If he is aware of these principles and understands them thoroughly he can teach the whole individual with confidence. If he does not understand and apply these principles, time will be wasted and less learning will take place in a given period of time.

Creating a Desire to Learn

We have discussed the principle of motivation under the previous heading. However, since this is such an important principle, it deserves further discussion. One instructor expressed the importance of motivation to this extent: "My observation has convinced me that the basic thing in teaching is to get the interest of the student; if you get that you cannot stop them from learning, and if you don't get that, they won't learn no matter what you do."

Although this might be putting it very strongly, all experienced instructors realize that the interest of the student is indispensable in the learning process. The problem of the instructor is not only to arouse interest but to keep the interest that the students spontaneously have. How often have you entered a class very much interested in the subject to have the instructor kill that interest by his attitude and lack of enthusiasm?

Although we say that the instructor must motivate the student, the source of this desire to learn must come from within the student. The instructor can set the stage, provide certain conditions for learning and make his instruction interesting but the student must do the rest. The instructor must provide the instructional situation which will cause the student to want to learn.

Classes of Motives

The motives that keep the individual going in life are extremely varied but they may be divided into two classes. These are specific motives and general motives.

(1) *Specific Motives.*

A specific motive is one that is aroused by a single value or objective which alone can satisfy the motive; or which, if removed would also remove the motive. For example; The police officer who has become interested in fingerprinting has a motive for studying fingerprinting. Only by studying fingerprinting can this motive be satisfied. Nothing else can be substituted. The instructor is interested in creating this specific motive for each subject he teaches.

(2) *General Motives.*

A general motive is one that is applicable equally to a number of subjects, things or situations. For example: a patrolman is interested in becoming a sergeant or a lieutenant. He wants to do everything well so that his record will indicate that he is capable of performing the duties of a sergeant. Good grades in a specific subject are valuable for obtaining the end sought. The subject studied is merely a means to an end.

The instructor is interested not only in the specific

motives but must assist in developing the general motives of the individual.

Techniques to Motivate Students

The efforts of the instructor to motivate students will to great extent be determined by the student taught and the subject matter. There are, however, certain fundamental techniques that can be applied to help motivate the students. Some of these are as follows:

(1) *Define Objective.*

Students will have more desire to learn a specific subject if they know how this will be beneficial to them. The instructor must show how the subject being taught fits into the over-all training program and how this will be used by the police officer. The instructor must make the student feel that he needs this lesson. For example: in teaching the laws of arrest to police officers, the officer can be told that he will be subject to civil and criminal action if he does not follow the rules of arrest and that his personal safety will be in jeopardy. The instructor cannot assume that the student will recognize the need for this particular subject. Many of the subjects taught in the police field seem totally unrelated to the work of the police officer when the student first hears of these subjects.

(2) *Place the Responsibility on the Student for Learning.*

Students will learn more when they are to be held accountable for learning. The police officer who has been carefully selected will accept responsibility for learning. The instructor should let the student know from the very beginning that he will be responsible for learning what is being taught. It might be necessary to give frequent examinations to determine if the student is accepting the responsibility. In subject areas where it is practicable the student should be required to demonstrate the fact that he has learned the particular subject matter or skill being taught.

(3) *Use Student Participation.*

Probably no other single factor is more important to

keep the student interested and motivated as student participation. If the student feels that he is a part of the learning process his interest will be kept high. The instructor should plan his lesson so that the student can take more part even if just asking or answering a question.

(4) *Use Varied Teaching Methods.*

Interest on the part of the student is often lost if the instructor uses the same method of teaching all the time, especially if this method is talking. The student will be motivated to learn and his interest will be kept high if the instructor uses personal force and enthusiasm, uses examples and illustrations, and uses various types of training aids.

(5) *Make use of "Recognition."*

It is human nature to desire recognition. Even though one might argue that the student should be motivated to learn even if he is not recognized, there can be no argument that a student whose work is recognized is a better student. It cannot be argued that he will not pay more attention to the subject if his work is recognized. If the student in class correctly answers a question his correct answer should be recognized. This not only motivates him to further learning but motivates the other students. Too often the instructor points out only the mistakes that are made by the student and fails to recognize the good work of the student. The instructor when discussing the student's work should point out the favorable or good points of the student work and then lead into suggestions for improvement. If the instructor plans his work so that the student will be able to perform some worthwhile activity early in the training period, and the instructor recognizes this accomplishment, the student will be motivated to put forth more effort.

(6) *Use Competition.*

The spirit of competition motivates people in all walks of life in this country. Competition can also be used as a motivating factor in learning. The instructor should take advantage of this natural impulse to excell in various types of competition. To do better than some of the other students in the class is a strong drive which should be given intelligent guidance by the instructor. The instructor should, however, be alert not to carry this personal competition to extremes. If one person in the class is consistently at the bottom of the class in grades or in other types of competitive examinations he will not be motivated to learn further but will in fact, in some instances, be less inclined to learn.

Probably the healthiest form of competition is competition with one's own record. The instructor should encourage the student to always strive to increase his record. As the golfer strives to increase his ability and thereby decrease the number of strokes, the student should be encouraged to attempt to beat his old record.

Another form of competition that can be utilized by the instructor is friendly competition between two or more groups or teams. This can be done in the police field by such things as mock crime investigations, role playing incidents, and firearms competition.

(7) *Give Rewards for Good Work.*

A less desirable means of motivation is the presenting of rewards to outstanding students. These have shown to be powerful incentives but often cause the student to seek high grades only for the purpose of these rewards rather than the real purpose of the training.

(8) *Use Punishment when other Means Fail.*

The least desirable technique of motivation is punishment. It should be used by the instructor only as the last resort. This negative approach to motivation often breeds resentment, antagonism, and the desire to avoid the form of learning to which it is attached.

We have indicated some of the techniques that the instructor can use to motivate students. The instructor who is aware of the necessity of motivation is limited in the techniques of motivation only by the degree of imagination and ingenuity he uses.

CLOSING

Summary

In this chapter the fundamental aspects of teaching and learning have been discussed.

a. *Learning* is defined as the process of acquiring new skills, new knowledge, techniques and appreciation which will enable the individual to do something he could not do before.

b. *Instruction* is defined as the sum of all the instructor activities contributing toward leading, guiding and directing and controlling the thoughts and actions of the students as they learn.

c. The *channels of learning* are the senses of sight, hearing, touch, smell, and taste. Through these channels ideas reach the mind and new learning takes place.

d. *Types of Learning.* Although we cannot make learning so stereotyped that it will fall exclusively into one of the types mentioned, the types of learning, if clearly understood by the instructor, will help him in deciding what method of teaching, or instruction, should be used. These types of learning are knowledge, skills, techniques, and appreciations.

e. *Certain principles of learning* must be known by the instructor in order for that instructor to teach subject matter efficiently and effectively. These principles are motivation, purpose, adjustment, activity, association, realism, and incidental learning. These are not the only principles of learning but these principles, if understood by the instructor, will assist the instructor in planning his lesson.

f. *Creating a Desire to Learn.* The student will learn much better if he has a desire to learn. The instructor can help create this desire by following certain techniques which will help motivate the students. These are defining the objective, placing the responsibility on the student for learning, encouraging participation by the student, varying the teaching techniques and methods, giving recognition to the student for answers, encouraging competition, offering rewards, and the least desirable, punishing the student. These techniques are only some of the techniques that can be used to motivate the student. The instructor who is thoughtful and ingenious will devise other techniques of motivation.

Closing Statement

The instructor is primarily interested in the development of students under his direction. This development will take place more readily if the instructor is familiar with the types of learning, the principles of learning, and the methods of creating a desire to learn within the students.

"If the student failed to learn, the instructor failed to teach."

Chapter 3

PLANNING FOR LEARNING ACTIVITIES
INTRODUCTION
Reasons for Chapter

Although actual teaching does not begin until the presentation stage of instruction, careful planning is the first step in efficient training. A plan is necessary in any endeavour. Before a contractor starts building a house he must have definite plans to be followed. Plans are necessary in every phase of police work. Planning is especially necessary for the police instructor. Teaching success depends more on lesson planning than it does on voice, personality, or even basic knowledge of the subject. The successful instructor, must first plan his lesson.

Objectives of Chapter

In this chapter we shall discuss the steps that must be followed by an instructor in planning for learning activities. We shall also consider a check list that can be used by the instructor in his planning.

Review of Previous Instruction

In our first chapter on foundations for learning we discussed the development process. We listed there several stages of instruction the instructor should be familiar with in organizing and presenting his material. The first stage mentioned was the preparation stage or planning stage. This is the stage of instruction which will be discussed in this chapter. Other stages of instruction will be discussed in later chapters.

Procedure

This chapter is divided into two basic parts. The discussion will first consider the steps in planning for learning activities; then the check list which can be used by an instructor in planning for student activities.

BODY

Steps in Planning for Learning Activities

The steps discussed here, if followed by the instructor, will assure the instructor that he has planned his lesson well. Although there is some overlapping in these steps and they could, in some instances, be in a different sequence, these steps will assist the instructor in reaching his desired goal; effective learning on the part of the student.

Determine Objectives of Whole Learning Activity

The first step for the instructor is to determine what his mission is, that is, what does he want the student to learn. What is he trying to accomplish in this series of lessons? Too often instructors start talking without having any aim or goal to be reached. The first step of the instructor should be to state in specific terms what he expects to accomplish in increasing the knowledge or improving the skills of the student. For example, if a police instructor is assigned the responsibility of teaching a recruit class the laws of arrest, he should immediately ask himself, just what am I to accomplish in teaching this course to this specific group?

Consult and Study All Reference Material

Probably the most logical second step in preparing a lesson in any subject is to consult and study all of the reference material available. Although the instructor might have had much experience in the field he will be teaching, it is usually, if not always, necessary to read additional material on this subject to be sure that all the points will be covered in the lesson. While reading the material, it is a good idea for the instructor to jot down on a pad the points he feels are important and should be considered. Too often, the instructor will say, "I know the subject matter," and he will make no further reference study.

Analyze the Material and Determine Logical Learning Units

After the instructor has determined the specific objectives he is to reach and has studied the reference material on this subject, the next step is to analyze the material and to determine the logical learning units. The instructor must decide how to organize the teaching points into major topics and sub-topics. For example, the instructor we mentioned earlier who had been assigned the responsibility of teaching the laws of arrest, after reading the subject matter over carefully will have decided that there are certain points that must be covered. He could decide that the main topics to be covered are (1) detention without arrest, (2) arrest without a warrant, (3) arrest with a warrant, (4) the amount of force that can be used in making an arrest, etc. Each of these then would have to be broken down further: the arrest without a warrant would have to be broken down into arrest for a misdemeanor without a warrant and arrest for a felony without a warrant.

The student will learn better if the topic headings are properly designated and the student is aware at all times of the topic which is being discussed.

Determine Sequence of Presenting Material

A consideration which is often overlooked by the police instructor is the sequence of presenting material. The material should be presented in a logical sequence, that is, the most simple material should be presented first and the more difficult material later as the student learns the basic material. In other words, the instructor should go from the simple to the complex. If the basic or more simple material is presented first, the student will have some background on which to base further learning.

Evaluate Factors Which will Affect Planning

At some time in his planning, the instructor must give careful consideration to factors which will affect his planning. All of these must be very carefully considered by the instructor before his final lesson plan is made. Some of these factors are:

(1) *Time available.*

In most police training schools time assigned to the instructor is limited. The instructor must plan to use this time effectively and efficiently keeping in mind his objective for the course. He must determine which of the learning units can be presented and how much time can be used for each of these. He must ask himself, should I present all of these units rapidly or should I spend more time on units which must be learned well? This is where the experience of the instructor can help him in deciding how much time to give to the various learning units. Lack of time can not justify poor instruction. The time factor will determine if class participation can be used, if supporting material can be included, or if the instructor can repeat the material often.

(2) *Training conditions.*

In some subject matter such as the teaching of firearms, the instructor must recognize that the weather might change and that it might be necessary to move indoors for the training period. He must therefore make his lesson plan flexible.

(3) *Assistant instructors available.*

In determining what and how to teach, it is obvious that planning will be affected by the availability of the assistant instructors. If assistant instructors are available, he might decide to divide his class into sections for more personal attention.

(4) *Equipment and facilities.*

The instructor will be limited in teaching certain subjects if he does not have the facilities and the equipment for teaching the subjects. Often it is necessary for the instructor to improvize. This cannot be a last minute arrangement.

(5) *State of training of students.*

One of the most important factors for the instructor to consider is the state of training of the student. As we indicated earlier the student learns by associating new material with past learning. The instructor should ask himself, do the students in this particular group have the necessary capacity and background training to learn this subject? Previous training of the students will, to a great extent, determine how much time the instructor must place on specific topics in his subjects.

The instructor must consider these factors and other factors and evaluate these factors carefully before presenting the material to the class.

Determine Method of Presenting Material

The method or combination of methods used by the instructor depends to a great extent on some of the factors we have already discussed, such as the time available, the equipment and facilities available, state of training of the students and how thoroughly the material should be learned. For example, if the material should be learned very thoroughly and the time is available, the conference method would be used rather than the lecture method. Also in determining the method to be used, the instructor must consider the size of the group. A subsequent chapter will go more thoroughly into this. At this point it is necessary to remind the instructor that one step in the planning is that the method of presentation must be determined before making the formal lesson plan.

Make the Formal Lesson Plan

After the previous steps have been followed, the instructor is ready to make the lesson plan. A later chapter will be devoted to making a formal lesson plan and will include the elements of the lesson plan and a sample lesson plan. The lesson plan should not be made until the instructor has answered the other questions indicated and has taken all the steps to this point. Before the actual lesson plan is made, the instructor should have determined *what* he intends to cover in this lesson, *why* he is teaching this material, and *how* the lesson will be presented.

Secure Aids and Facilities Needed

After a lesson plan has been made, the instructor will determine what training aids and what facilities will be needed to present the lesson effectively. The facilities should be requested early and the aids made at an early date in order to be sure that they will be available when needed. When the instructor has very little time to prepare his lesson, it is a good idea to determine what aids are needed early in the lesson planning even before the lesson plan has been made, in order that he can be sure of having the necessary aids and facilities.

A later chapter will be devoted to the use of training aids. The instructor must remember, however, that in planning his lesson, to a great extent, the success of his teaching will be dependent upon the aids and facilities he has available.

Rehearse the Lesson

One might think he has finished when lesson plan had been completed and the aids and facilities ordered. However, there are other steps the instructor should take before the presenting of the material to the class. One of these is that the instructor should completely rehearse the lesson. Too often, the instructor finds during the actual presentation that he has allowed too much time or not enough time for the presentation or that the lesson plan is lacking in some respect. The instructor should always accept the fact that it is his responsibility to use the time he has allotted as efficiently as is possible.

As there will be no further discussion on this phase, some points to apply when rehearsing the lesson are indicated here.

(1) *The rehearsal should be complete in every respect.*

In order for the timing to be as closely worked out as possible and in order for the instructor to use his training aids effectively, the instruction should include the use of all training aids, demonstrations and examinations if the examination is to be used. The physical set up should be as close to the actual situation as possible. Also if assistants are to be used in presentation, they should also be used in the rehearsal.

(2) *The rehearsal should be before another instructor.*

Recognizing that the instructor wants to do the very best possible job when he is presenting the material to the class, he should have another instructor present when he rehearses. The rehearsal presentation should be conducted in a formal and serious manner. The instructor might at first have some hesitancy in presenting a lesson to a one-man class, however if it is understood that he is rehearsing the lesson in order to improve his technique, a critique of his instruction by another instructor will be very beneficial. Often another instructor can point out ways in which the instruction could be improved both from a content standpoint and from the standpoint of method of instruction.

(3) *The lesson should be rehearsed before each class presentation.*

Once the lesson plan has been made, the instructor can generally use this lesson plan in several presentations in the course of a year. If, however, the instructor has waited some time before presenting the material to a new class he should rehearse the lesson again. Unless the instructor has a phenominal memory, he will not be able to remember all the details he had planned to present to this class. Even if the instructor has presented the plan recently, it is always a good idea to "talk through" the lesson to himself before presenting the lesson to the class. This will refresh his memory as to the points to be presented.

Check Plan and Facilities Before Class Starts.

Planning for learning activities continues right up to the time class is scheduled to start. Just as the basketball coach makes sure everything is ready before he puts his team on the floor, the instructor must make a final check to see if everything is ready before he starts his instruction. Before starting the class, the instructor should take some time to check the following:

(1) *The Lesson Plan.*

The instructor should be sure he has the correct lesson plan for this subject and the lesson plan in such a condition that it can be used efficiently.

(2) *Equipment.*

The instructor should make certain he has all of the equipment that is necessary in this particular lesson. He should see that the physical set up is properly arranged, the lighting is sufficient, the ventilation properly adjusted.

(3) *Training Aids.*

The instructor must check to determine if he has the correct training aids, and if they are arranged in the sequence in which they are to be used.

(4) *Instructional Material.*

The instructor should be sure that all the instructional materials for the student's use are on hand.

(5) *Assistants.*

If assistants are to be used, the instructor should

determine if all of the assistants are prepared and available.

These steps, if followed by the instructor, will assist him in preparing his lesson in such a way that the time allotted for this instruction can be used as efficiently as possible.

A Check List on Planning

Planning to a great extent depends upon the instructor, the type of material to be presented, the level of the class, the material to be presented, and the time authorized for the presentation. This check list can be generally used in all types of lesson plans. It helps the instructor feel secure in the knowledge that he has done a good job of planning. The instructor should ask himself these questions after he has completed his planning.

a. Am I sure in my own mind what the objective of this course is?

b. Have I properly reviewed the pertinent reference material concerning this subject matter?

c. Have I selected the important teaching points and broken these points down into logical titles and sub titles?

d. Have I arranged the material in such sequence that it will have meaning to the learner?

e. Can the ideas and procedures be mastered by the students in the allotted time?

f. Are the facts to be presented meaningful to the students at this stage of training?

g. Has the lesson been built on previous experiences and abilities of the students?

h. Has the importance of the lesson and the reasons for teaching it been brought out in terms of future requirements?

i. Is the method of presenting the material the most suitable for the students and the particular material to be learned?

j. Have I made my lesson plan so complete that no points will be missed?

   k. Have training aids been properly selected to assist in putting over ideas to the students?

   l. Have plans been made for class participation?

   m. Have plans been made to emphasize the important parts in the lesson?

   n. Is everything in readiness in the classroom?

   o. Have materials for evaluation been provided and standards of performance been determined?

CLOSING

Summary

In this chapter we have discussed the first stage of the instructional process, that is, the planning or preparation stage. We have indicated there are 10 basic steps that the instructor must generally follow while planning learning activities. These steps are as follows:

   a. Determine the objective of the whole learning activity.

   b. Consult and study reference material.

   c. Analyze the material and determine the logical learning units.

   d. Determine sequence of presenting material.

   e. Evaluate the factors which will affect the planning.

   f. Determine the methods of presenting the material.

   g. Make the formal lesson plan.

   h. Secure aids and facilities needed.

   i. Rehearse the lesson.

   j. Check plans and facilities before the class starts.

We also discussed in this chapter a check list that the instructor can use in evaluating his planning for the student activity.

Closing Statement

Careful planning is always the first and most important stage of planning. Careful preliminary analysis, the correct solution of all instructional problems and repeated rehearsal and review of procedures and material, should insure the transfer of knowledge and skill to the student in a minimum of time. It should also insure the instructor's self confidence and ease.

In nearly every case, the student's failure to learn can be traced to the instructor's inadequate planning.

Chapter 4

PHASES OF ORAL INSTRUCTION
INTRODUCTION
Reasons for Chapter

W hatever the method used by the instructor in presenting his material to the class, the material must be properly organized. The purpose of this chapter is to discuss the various phases of the oral instruction in order that the instructor may not only present ideas but make it possible for the students to express the ideas in deeds and actions.

Objectives of Chapter

The objectives of this chapter is to teach the student the three phases of oral instruction. These are the "introduction," the "body," and the "closing" phases.

Review of Previous Instruction

In an earlier chapter we discussed the stages of instruction. We said the first stage of instruction was the presentation stage. After the lesson has been prepared, it must be presented. In this chapter we shall discuss this stage of instruction; the presentation stage.

Procedure

In this chapter we shall first discuss the "introduction" and the parts which should be included in the "introduction"; secondly, the "body"; its purposes and contents; and thirdly, the "closing."

BODY

As we indicated in our introduction to this chapter, oral instruction is generally in three phases. One authority on education said, "We tell 'em what we're going to tell 'em, we tell 'em, and we tell 'em what we told 'em." To put this in a little more dignified wording, we say the oral instruction is divided into the "introduction," the "body" and the "closing." The instructor's task is simplified and his instruction is more effective, if he understands how each of these elements is employed.

The "Introduction" as a Phase of Oral Instruction

Purposes of the Introduction

The introduction has a real purpose. It sets the stage for the instructor's presentation. It puts the student in the proper frame of mind to receive the instruction. Some of the more specific purposes then, of the introduction, are as follows:

(1) *To establish contact with the class.*

Often the student is in the classroom in body but his mind is far away thinking of something entirely foreign to the subject matter. In order for there to be a transfer of knowledge from the instructor to the student there must be constant contact between the instructor and the sudent. Some methods of establishing this contact are:

(a) Use a good opening statement.

For example, the instructor who is teaching the elements of various crimes could open his class with the statement, "Before the officer can enforce the law, he must know the law."

(b) Refer to a matter of special interest to this class or to an idea which is dominant at the moment.

(c) Compliment the class or express the pleasure of the instructor at something the class has done.

(d) Open with a story which is directly related to the lesson being taught.

(e) Use a rhetorical question; a question which stimulates interest but from which you expect no answer.

(f) Have a skit or a demonstration directly related to this subject.

(2) *To motivate the students to learn.*

Another purpose of the introduction is to motivate the students. Instructors, not only in police schools, but in high schools and grade schools often fail because they have not motivated the students. We cannot assume that the student will recognize the value of this particular subject. The responsibility is on the instructor to create a desire on the part of the student to learn this particular lesson. The methods we spoke of above to establish contact with the class will also often motivate the student to learn, that is, the use of skits, demonstrations and stories directly related to the subject. A good way to motivate the student to learn is to give an actual case wherein a police officer has made use of the material being taught.

(3) *To disclose subject matter and procedure.*

The student in the police school will learn better if he knows *what* is to be taught, *how* it is to be taught, and *why* the subject is to be taught. The student will be with the instructor more if he has been told in advance the order in which the teaching points will be presented. Also the student should be taught how this part of the instruction fits in with the previous instruction and how this will fit into the overall instructional objective.

Elements of the Introduction

We have discussed under "Purposes of the Introduction" above some of the purposes or reasons for having an introduction in oral instruction. To be certain these purposes are accomplished in the introduction, a list of elements which should be considered by the instructor in preparing his introduction are here discussed. Not all lesson plans will have all of these elements but each of them should be considered. *Each* lesson plan should have the *reasons* for the lesson and the *objectives* of the lesson.

(1) *Reasons for the lesson.*

The student will learn more if he knows why the lesson is to be presented. The instructor should make the reasons convincing and use real life illustrations and examples where possible. Often the student is unable to imagine how the material can be used at a later time. The instructor must motivate the student to learn by pointing out to him how this material will help him at the present or in the future.

(2) *Objectives of lesson.*

Somewhat related to the reasons for learning the lesson is the element of "objective." The instructor under this element of introduction should state briefly and concisely what is to be learned in this lesson. In doing this he should place responsibility on the class for learning rather than on the instructor. For example, he should say, "*We* will learn the fundamentals of fingerprinting" rather than "*I* will teach you the fundamentals of fingerprinting." He should be certain that his objective is stated briefly, clearly, decisively, and specifically. The objectives should also be stated forcefully and enthusiastically as the attitude of the instructor will "carry over" to the students. Some instructors start the class with a phrase such as this, "This is a dry subject but I have been assigned to teach it, so bear with me." With this attitude the instructor can expect very little learning on the part of the student.

(3) *Review of previous instruction.*

Where the lesson being presented is part of a larger subject, the instructor will secure the attention of the student more and have the students "with him" if he reviews briefly the previous lessons and ties this lesson in with those previously presented and those which are to be presented in the future. This brief review makes the student "at home," realizing that he has learned something and that this is a continuation of previous learning. The review also re-emphasizes the important points which have been taught prior to this lesson. This applies the principle of learning by repitition.

(4) *Procedures.*

Keeping in mind that the instructor wants the student to know exactly what will be covered and how it is to be covered, the instructor should briefly state the procedure to be followed.

These are the four elements that should be considered by the instructor for the introduction. Some instructors like to add another element which specifies the standards expected of the student. As pointed out, not all of these are necessarily included in every period of oral instruction. For example, if there has been no instruction in this subject up to this point, there will be no review of previous instruction. Or the instructor might find it unnecessary to specify the procedure when it is obvious. Generally speaking, if these elements are included, the lesson will be off to a good start.

The "Body" as a Phase of Oral Instruction

In the body of the lesson or the explanation phase of the lesson, the actual teaching points are presented to the student. In the introduction, the instructor has told the students what he is going to teach and in the body he actually presents the teaching points, develops understanding and stimulates appreciations.

Purposes of the Body

Some of the specific purposes of the body of the lesson are as follows:

(1) *To present teaching points.*

The instructor has determined in his planning that there are certain teaching points the student must know in order to perform his duties efficiently. The first objective of the instructor then, is to present these teaching points.

(2) *To develop understanding.*

The instructor has the responsibility of not only presenting teaching points but helping the student to understand these teaching points. Everything the instructor does; his words, his actions, his attitude, helps the students in developing understanding. This is all a part of teaching.

(3) *To stimulate appreciations.*

Not only must the student have been presented the teaching points and understand them, he must develop attitudes and appreciations which will help him in applying the material being taught. For example, the student may have been taught the laws of arrest but unless he has developed appreciations in the applications of these laws, very little has been accomplished. To a great extent, it is not what the teacher or instructor says, but how he says it. It is very easy for the instructor to present teaching points but it is very difficult to develop those appreciations which must be developed in order for there to be complete learning. The instructor must realize that his voice, his words, his attitude and even his dress will have some effect in developing appreciations on the part of the student.

Principles to be Followed in Presenting the Material

Some of the principles which will be of value to the instructor in presenting his material are listed here. These principles should be considered by the instructor.

(1) *Presentation must be organized.*

Have you ever been in a class where the instructor digressed to such an extent and jumped from point to point so rapidly that you spent most of your time trying to keep your notes organized and missed out on much of the material being presented? The organization of the lesson will have been determined in the planning stage. The careful instructor has organized the material in such a way that the student can follow it easily. This planning, however, will be of no value if the instructor fails to follow the procedure he has decided upon. The instructor must therefore follow the lesson plan in presenting the teaching points. The student will be aided greatly in following the organization if the instructor uses the blackboard, charts or other types of training aids to show the points which are being discussed and presented. The instructor can also help the student by giving the student, previous to the class period, an outline of the instruction or what is sometime called an advance sheet. The student will not be able to achieve the learning objective if he has not been able to follow the instructor.

(2) *Make transitions from one point to another point smoothly.*

A well presented lesson progresses by steps. When presented smoothly, the parts are connected by transitional words or statements. A smooth transition from one point to another makes it easier for the student to follow the instruction and to know when one point is finished and the next point is taken up. Some of the methods or techniques to be followed in making the transition from one point to another are as follows:

(a) Refer often to the objectives of the lesson.

If the objectives have been clearly designated, the instructor can go from one objective to the other, letting the student know that one objective has been discussed and the instructor is now going to the second objective.

(b) Use frequent summaries.

The use of the summary within the lesson accomplishes two purposes. First, it emphasizes the teaching points which have been covered, and secondly, it lets the student know that the instructor is now going to a different point.

(c) Use rhetorical questions.

The instructor can get from one point to another point by asking the class a question which would lead into the next point. For example, if the instructor is teaching the principles of learning, he could say, "We have discussed two of the principles of learning, what is the third principle of learning?" In this type of question, the instructor does not necessarily expect a definite answer from the class but only stimulates their thinking and lets them know that he is going to another teaching point.

(d) Use connective words or phrases.

Another method of going smoothly from one point to another is to use connective words, such as "however," "moreover," "therefore," "accordingly," etc. The instructor must be careful that he does not "overwork" any of these words or phrases.

(e) Use charts and other training aids.

One of the best ways to let the student know you are going to another point is to use a chart with the teaching points listed or some type of other aid which can be projected upon the screen, showing the teaching points and indicating that you have completed one point and are now going to another. In our chapter on the use of training aids we will have some suggestions for the instructor on how to use training aids to accomplish this purpose.

(3) *Keep interest and attention of the students.*

It is the instructor's responsibility to keep the interest and attention of the students. This is a real challenge to the instructor, especially in some types of subject matter and at certain periods during the day. When the instructor merely talks without doing something else to maintain student interest, the interest will soon die. To keep the classes alive and to promote learning, the instructor should consider some of the following suggestions.

(a) Use stories and experiences.

The police instructor who has field experiences will generally be able to maintain interest better than the instructor who has not. The stories and experiences which bring out the points being taught should be directly related to the teaching points. An example of how this teaching point has been applied or has not been applied in the past will often alert the class to the instruction.

(b) Be specific.

The instructor should avoid talking in vague or general terms as the class often loses interest. If the instructor is very specific as to his teaching points, however, and is very definite as to what the teaching points are, the class will be more interested and pay attention.

(c) Use training aids.

One of the best methods of maintaining the interest of the student and keeping his attention is to use various types of training aids. Some types of training aids can be used in every type of presentation. For example; charts, diagrams, and models can be used to keep the interest of the students and to bring about better learning. The instructor should plan to use the training aids at all points in the oral presentation when the lesson may seem dull.

(d) Use questions.

In a later chapter we will discuss the use of questions and how questions should be directed to the students. One of the best ways of maintaining interest and attention of the class is to use questions and let the students participate.

(4) *Make use of analogies.*

In presenting material to the class, the instructor must remember that the material is generally new to the students. The instructor can help the students to learn this new material which is about to be revealed to him by the use of the analogy. The instructor links something strange with something familiar. For example, we describe the shape of the earth as being like a big ball. Throughout life, analogies become one of the key methods by which new ideas and concepts are developed. The instructor, of course, must make use of this principle.

(5) *Emphasize teaching points.*

Emphasis is another principle which must be followed by the instructor in presenting his material. The instructor, in his planning, has determined that there are certain definite teaching points which must be presented to this class. Throughout the presentation, the instructor must emphasize these points by repetition, frequent summaries, and by voice inflection in order to be sure that the student has obtained these teaching points. It is best not to emphasize or repeat an idea immediately after its first presentation. The best results are reached when the instructor waits a few minutes and then repeats or reviews the teaching points. The emphasis must be planned and distributed properly or it will become monotonous.

(6) *Teach the students as well as the subject matter.*

The student is not only learning the teaching points being presented but he is developing understanding and appreciations. Everything the instructor does which helps the student to learn is part of the teaching. The instructor must, therefore, be a leader as well as an instructor. In carrying out this principle, the instructor must apply the fundamental principles which we discussed in Chapter 1.

The "Closing" as a Phase of Oral Instruction

We have indicated that the "introduction" is the first phase of oral instruction. In the introduction the student was told what would be presented in the body. The second phase of the oral instruction is the "body." The third phase of the oral instruction is the "closing." This is sometimes called the summary. The word "closing" is probably better, however, as the summary is used throughout the instruction. The closing, as do the other two phases of oral instruction, has a very definite purpose. The instructor should be skilled in the use of the closing phase and know what it contains and how it is used most effectively. In the closing, the instructor has an opportunity to wrap up the lesson in a complete package for the students. The purposes and the elements of the closing are discussed below.

Purposes of the Closing

Give over-all view.

In the closing, the instructor has an opportunity to tie together all of the teaching points which were presented in the lesson. The instructor has probably presented many varied teaching points and there is a good possibility that the student has not tied all of these points together so that he will get an over-all view. In the closing, the student should be given an opportunity to complete the pattern; to take parts which have been thoroughly developed and fit them into a whole pattern. This closing or final summary helps the student to find a firm basis for performance.

To Emphasize Teaching Points.

In the closing, the instructor has an opportunity to again emphasize the important teaching points and ideas he has presented. This final review of the teaching points might be just what it takes to firmly fix these points in the mind of the student.

To Clarify Instruction and Answer Questions.

In the closing phase of the oral instruction, the instructor should give students an opportunity to ask questions on points which may be clear to them. The instructor wants the students to leave the classroom with a clear conception of the teaching points presented. If there have been questions in the minds of the students, the instructor, in the closing, will have an opportunity to clarify his instruction so that the student will have no doubts in his mind as to what his instructor intended for him to learn.

Elements of the Closing

To accomplish the purposes of the closing as we indicated above, there are certain elements which should be considered by the instructor to be included in the closing.

Question Opportunity.

So that there will be no question in the mind of the student, probably the first thing the instructor should consider in his closing is the opportunity for the students to ask questions. If the instructor has given this opportunity to the students during the class, there will probably not be very many questions at this point. The questions would probably concern the tying together of the teaching points rather than the teaching points themselves. However, the instructor should let the students have this opportunity to clear up *any* questions he has in mind.

Summary of Points Presented.

In the closing, the instructor should briefly summarize the points which have been presented in the class. This not only emphasizes the teaching points but ties these points together in an understandable unit.

Closing Statement

The lesson should be closed as carefully as it opened. A statement used by the instructor should be carefully thought out and have a specific purpose. The closing statement should leave a lasting impression in the minds of the students concerning the subject. The closing statement should make the student feel as if he has learned something about the subject and should be related to the objectives of the lesson.

CLOSING

Summary

In this chapter we have discussed the three phases of oral

instruction. These are the *introduction, the body,* and the *closing.* We have learned that each of these phases of oral instruction has a definite purpose and each should be carefully considered by the instructor.

Closing Statement

Regardless of the method the instructor has chosen to present the oral instruction, he will feel more confident and the student will learn more effectively if he follows a definite plan in presenting his instruction. The instructor must present the material effectively and efficiently, recognizing that the student has given him his most precious possession — his time.

Chapter 5

METHODS OF PRESENTING INSTRUCTION
INTRODUCTION

Reasons for Chapter

In order for the instructor to develop learning on the part of the student, he must be familiar with the various methods which can be used to aid the student in learning. The instructor who is familiar with these methods of presenting instruction and has the ability to select the best method, will have greater success than the instructor who does not plan his approach to instruction.

Objectives of Chapter

In this chapter, the methods of presenting instruction will be discussed as well as the advantages and disadvantages of the various methods of presenting instruction to the students.

Review of Previous Instruction

In an earlier chapter, we discussed the steps in presenting material, stating that the first step was to plan the lesson. In the fourth chapter, we discussed the phases of oral instruction. Continuing our discussion of presenting material to the class, we shall, in this chapter, discuss the methods that can be used by the instructor in presenting material.

Procedure

We shall first discuss the advantages of the lecture method of presenting instruction, secondly the conference method, and thirdly the demonstration method of presenting instruction.

BODY

Before the instructor presents material to the class or assists the student in learning, he must determine the method he will use in presenting the teaching points. The instructor may use many different methods or combinations of methods in accomplishing his purpose. Methods of presenting instruction to the class are generally divided into three categories, the lecture method, the conference method, and the demonstration method. To a great extent, the size of the class and the type of subject matter presented will determine the method used by the instructor or the combination of methods the instructor will use.

In the following paragraphs we shall discuss each of these three methods, the disadvantages of each method, the advantages of each method and the principles to be applied in each of these methods.

Lecture Method

In the lecture method of instruction, the instructor develops his subject matter entirely by himself without class participation and without giving the class the opportunity to ask questions. The lecture method has some advantages but also has some disadvantages. In order that the instructor may determine whether he will use the lecture method or not, it is necessary to point out some of the advantages and disadvantages.

Advantages

(1) *The material can be presented to a large class.* The lecture method is sometimes the only method that can be used in presenting instruction. If the class is large and the student cannot make himself heard from every part of the classroom, it is difficult to use any other method.

(2) *Many ideas may be presented in a short time.*

The instructor can cover a large amount of material in a short period by the use of the lecture method. He must determine how much material he must cover and how well the student must know the material. He must recognize the fact that if he covers many points by the use of the lecture method in a short time, the students will not learn these points as well as they would if the points were covered by a different method. The instructor can often determine which method he will use in presenting the material by thinking of the bulls eye of instruction. In the center of the bulls eye, is the material the student *must* know. Within the second circle is the material the student *should* know and within the third circle of the bullseye of instruction is the material that it *would be well* for the students to know.

(3) *Basic material can be presented in a short time.*

With the lecture method, facts and principles needed to provide a common background can be presented in a short time.

Often, it is necessary to present this material so that the class will have a background on which to base further learning.

(4) *Other methods can be introduced.*

One advantage of the lecture method is that it can be used to introduce other methods. For example, before practical work is given to the students or before a demonstration is made, the instructor might start out with a lecture to introduce the demonstration and to set the stage for the practical work.

(5) *Materials may be summarized rapidly.*

In some instances where the students are fairly well acquainted with the material, the lecture method can be used to summarize the material.

Disadvantages

(1) *Students can not ask questions.*

Probably the greatest disadvantage of the straight lecture method is that the students can not ask questions. The student trying to understand the material being presented may have a question on some point. If he is unable to clarify that point, the rest of the instruction could have little meaning.

(2) *Students lose interest.*

Often where the material is being presented by the straight lecture method, the student loses interest and does not learn the teaching points. Of course, the good lecturer to some extent can overcome this by adding interesting stories or presenting the material in a more interesting manner.

(3) *Too many ideas are often presented.*

Normally, in the strict lecture method, so many ideas are presented that it is impossible for the student to completely comprehend all of the ideas. As pointed out earlier, the instructor must consider this and determine the method he will use to achieve his purpose.

(4) *Only one of the five senses is used.*

Generally speaking if the lecture method is used exclusively, only one of the five of the senses is used; the sense of hearing. Tests have proved that when only the scnse of hearing is used, only a small percentage of the material is retained by the students. To some extent, this objection or disadvantage can be overcome if the material is not given too rapidly and the students are allowed to take notes.

Principles to be Followed

In presenting material by the lecture method, there are certain principles which, if followed by the instructor, will help the student learn the teaching points. Some of these principles are as follows:

(1) *Be sure lecture is organized.*

The lecturer who jumps from one subject to another without any organization soon "loses" the student. The lecture should be organized logically and progressively.

(2) *Make points specific and clear.*

The instructor who has determined in advance the teaching points he must cover in this class will make these teaching points specific and try to make them clearly understood by the student. Talking in generalities often confuses the student, leaves him with little understanding as to what the teaching points are.

(3) *Use words that can be understood by the student.*

Simple one or two-syllable words pack much more punch than four-bit jaw-busters. The lecturer must ask himself, do the students understand the words I am using in communicating with them?

(4) *Do not present too many ideas in a short time.*

If the instructor expects the student to actually learn and remember the teaching points, he must remember that he cannot present too many teaching points in a short time.

(5) *Keep the interest of the students.*

If the instructor is to develop ideas and attitudes on the part of the student, he must keep their interest. This can be done by using stories, examples, displaying interest and being active in the presentation.

(6) *Summarize the teaching points.*

Frequent summaries used throughout the lecture will help emphasize the teaching points and keep the students more alert.

(7) *Use good speech techniques.*

The lecturer must apply good speech techniques. He must speak clearly, loudly enough to be heard, enunciate clearly and be enthusiastic in his presentation. If the instructor has not had a course in public speaking or effective communication he should study carefully one of the many good books on this subject.

Conference Method

As we indicated earlier, one of the methods of presenting material is the Conference or Discussion Method. As pointed out also, classification of instruction into the three methods is not too accurate because there is usually no sharp distinction between these methods and the instructor often used several methods during one period of instruction. The classification of methods, however, does serve a useful purpose as the instructor can determine which method will be predominant. No label can completely describe what the instructor is doing.

A conference type activity, often called the discussion method, includes all activities which tend to develop an interchange of ideas between the instructor and the students and between the students. A mutual interchange of experience and thought takes place with the objective being the solution of a problem or the development of a logical conclusion. There are many variations of the Conference Method and the instructor must choose the one which will develop learning best. Some of the techniques included within this category are as follows:

Instructor Dominated

Close to the lecture method of presentation is the instructor-dominated technique of presenting material. Here the instructor presents the material to the class much as in the lecture method but allows the members of the class to ask questions as they desire and the instructor to ask questions of the class.

Seminar or Group Discussion

In the seminar or group discussion the instructor acts as a moderator or a discussion leader. The instructor participates only for motivation and guidance purposes. For this type of learning to be effective in the development of the student, the student must take an active part. In the discussion, questions should come from the student and for the most part be answered by the student. A group discussion may be thought of as an orderly conversation among the students and between the students and the instructor, directed toward attaining a definite objective.

Panel

Another technique which is included in the Conference Method of instruction is the use of the student panel. Various members of the class are selected and assigned basic topics to discuss. The instructor here acts only as a guide and keeps the discussion directed toward the goal. The class may be authorized to participate by asking questions of the panel or the panel members may keep the discussion among themselves.

In the Conference Method of instruction, there are advantages and disadvantages. These advantages and disadvantages are discussed on the following pages.

Advantages

(1) *Student has an opportunity to ask questions.*

One of the greatest advantages of the conference method is that the student is given an opportunity to clarify the points he does not understand. This develops a better understanding of the material being taught.

(2) *It increases student interest and keeps the student more alert.*

If the student is given an opportunity to ask questions and is required to answer questions, he will be kept more alert and participate more actively in the instruction.

(3) *It stimulates the thinking of the students.*

When the students are required to participate and expected to participate, their thinking is stimulated more than if they were only required to sit in the class and listen.

(4) *Material is learned more thoroughly.*

Because the student is allowed to participate and is required to think and take part in the discussion, he will work out the problems in his own mind and will understand the teaching points more thoroughly.

(5) *It gives the instructor the opportunity to correct misconceptions.*

With the student participation, the instructor can become more familiar with how much the student is learning as he goes along and can correct any misunderstandings or misconceptions concerning the material.

(6) *It enables an instructor to make use of background experiences of the students.*

Often the students in class, especially in classes of experienced police officers, have many experiences which will be of interest to other students. The conference method gives the instructor the opportunity to make use of these experiences.

(7) *It helps to develop a healthy group spirit.*

It gives the students an opportunity to discuss the material being presented, it helps them to understand the opinions of others, and develops a group spirit.

(8) *The material is retained longer.*

Not only will the students learn more of the teaching points, but they will retain the material longer if allowed to participate in the discussion.

Disadvantages

(1) *Cannot be used for a large class.*

One of the chief disadvantages of the conference method is that it cannot be used for a large class. It is preferable to have a class of twenty-five or less if the conference method is to be used. Some authorities set the limit at fifteen. It is obvious that there can be very little group discussion if the class is so large that some students can not be heard by other students. In this situation, many of the students will not be able to take part at all.

(2) *Fewer points can be presented.*

If a conference method is used, fewer points can be presented by the instructor. Here again, the instructor must determine how well the students must learn the teaching points. If the instructor desires that the teaching points be learned well, the conference method is preferable to the lecture method. If the class is allowed to discuss the points, to ask questions and to answer questions, the amount of material will be limited but the learning will be more thorough.

(3) *Time control is difficult.*

It is not too difficult for the instructor to time his presentation if he uses the lecture method as he can practice in advance and determine how long it will take. However, if the conference method is used, the instructor will not be able to accurately determine how much the class will participate or how long they will take on one teaching point. It might be necessary for the instructor to limit the discussion on a certain point in order to cover all of the teaching points.

(4) *Preparation is more difficult.*

At first glance it might seem that less preparation for the conference type is necessary. However, this is not true. The instructor preparing the strict lecture needs only to research the material he is actually presenting. In using the conference method of instruction, the instructor must not only know the material he is presenting to the class but have a complete understanding of the subject matter in order to keep discussion on the subject and to answer questions relative to the teaching points.

Principles to be Followed

If the conference method of instruction is to be effective, the instructor must keep in mind certain principles that he must follow. Some of these are:

(1) *Be prepared.*

More than in the lecture method of instruction, the instructor must prepare thoroughly. He must not only know the teaching points to be presented, but have a thorough understanding of all relative points, and a complete understanding of the subject matter.

(2) *Encourage participation.*

To be successful, and to stimulate learning on the part of the students, the instructor should try to get all of the students to participate. He should also take advantage of the experience and skill of the entire group. If the instructor is using a seminar or group discussion technique he should avoid dominating the discussion as much as is possible. The students should answer the questions but the instructor should check the accuracy of the answers and rephrase and elaborate when necessary. It is always a good idea to let other students answer questions if this is practical and the students have some knowledge of the subject matter being presented.

(4) *Summarize frequently.*

As points are discussed, the instructor must summarize and tie them in with previous instruction on this point. The students will have a tendency to get off the subject if the instructor does not constantly summarize and keep them aware of the objective of the lesson. At the end of the discussion, the instructor should make a summary of all important points and conclusions reached. If practical, the students should also participate in the summarization.

Use of Questions in Instruction

Questioning is not a method of teaching, however it is a valuable asset in teaching, especially when using the conference method. Often the difference between the passive absorption of information and the active learning is in proportion to the use of questions. The test of a good question is the extent to which it helps to attain the objectives of a particular lesson. In the following paragraphs we shall discuss the (1) Reasons for asking questions, (2) Characteristics of a good question, (3) Policies in asking a question and (4) Standards in student's answers.

(1) *Reasons for asking questions.*

(a) Increases student interest.

Students, when allowed to ask questions, and who are asked questions by the instructor feel that they are part of the presentation and therefore pay more attention to the instruction.

(b) Stimulates student thinking.

Questions stimulate the thinking, thereby helping the student to learn.

(c) Checks understanding.

Questions are the instructor's best check of the general level of his class. If the students consistently fail to answer his questions, this indicates that he must present certain material again, perhaps using a different approach. Questions also show misunderstandings which can be corrected on the spot and indicate student weaknesses to the instructor.

(d) Encourage student participation.

Questions give the students the opportunity to express their attitudes. A students' answers to questions often indicate his interest and attitude toward the training program, the instructor, and the subject matter. An instructor may desire to change his approach to make the student more ready to accept the material.

(e) Introduces class experiences.

Often the members of the class will have had experiences which will help the instructor in putting over his teaching points. This is especially true in classes of experienced police officers.

(f) Emphasizes the main points of the lesson.

The instructor who makes good use of questions, emphasizes the points he is teaching by questioning the students on these points. This will help the students recall and fix in their minds the important points of the lesson.

(g) Test the effectiveness of the instruction.

If the students are not able to answer the questions the instructor gives them, he should be aware that his teaching has been ineffective. Questions will reveal the specific areas where the instructor has been the least effective.

(2) *Characteristics of a good question.*

Recognizing that questions play a very important part in helping the student to learn, the instructor should prepare his questions before the class starts. Whether the key questions are prepared before the class starts or prepared during the class, here are some suggestions which should prove of value to the instructor.

(a) Questions should have a specific purpose.

An instructor should ask himself, "is this question to emphasize a major point, to stimulate thought, to arouse interest of the class, to determine if the class has learned a specific point, etc?" In preparing the lesson, an instructor should include questions in his lesson plan at the place that he would like to ask the questions for a specific purpose.

(b) Questions must be understood.

Questions should be phrased in language and terms familiar to the student. The wording of the question should be definite, clear, and concise. The students must know exactly what he is being asked and should have the same mental picture of what is wanted as the instructor.

(c) Questions should emphasize only one point.

The instructor should avoid asking two questions in

one or asking a question in such a way that several other questions are needed to bring out the information desired. Questions should require a definite answer. The instructor must state the question in such a way that a definite answer is required and in such a way that the students will not be tempted to bluff or to make a guess as to the correct answer.

(d) Questions should not suggest the answer.

The instructor should avoid leading questions or questions which suggest a "yes" or "no" answer.

(e) Questions should emphasize an understanding of relationships rather than a memorization of facts.

Questions that ask "how" or "why" require the student to analyze the situation and are generally preferred to questions as to "who," "what," "where," or "when," which are used only for recalling facts.

(3) *Policies in asking questions.*

(a) Address the question to the entire class before designating a student to answer.

If the question is directed to only one student, the rest of the class will relax and not concentrate on the question. However, if the question is asked before the student is called, all of the members of the class will be required to think about the question. The instructor should *ask the question, pause* to give the students an opportunity to think about the question, *call on the student* to answer the question, and finally *evaluate* the *answer.*

(b) Distribute questions fairly among the students.

The instructor should not confine his questioning to superior or interested students, or to students whose names are easy to pronounce. All students should be given an opportunity to participate. This does not mean, however, that the instructor will ask each student exactly the same number of questions or that he will follow a certain order in asking questions. The instructor who uses a seating chart and asks one question of one student and the next question of the next student, encourages the student to pay attention only when he is about to be called upon. The seating chart can be used to great advantage to insure that all students are questioned but it should not be used as a means of following a fixed order.

(c) Make questioning a part of the instruction.

Questions should not be a threat to students but should be asked in a natural, interested and conversational tone of voice. A student should not feel that the presentation has stopped after questioning has begun.

(4) *Standards in students' answers to questions.*

The instructor should require certain standards in the students' answers to questions.

(a) The student's answers should be heard by all of the class.

The instructor should tell the students to address their questions and answers to the class rather than to the instructor. To allow discussion, the student's answer must be heard and repeated if necessary by the instructor.

(b) Group answers should be avoided.

Generally, group answers should be avoided. The instructor gets better results by calling on individuals to answer certain questions. If group answers are allowed, those who answer loudly will cover up those who do not. There is a possible exception to this where the purpose of the question is to drill members of the class.

(c) Encourage students to answer the questions.

Often the timid student will say, "I don't know" to all questions, when in fact, he does know the answer to the questions but is hesitant to speak out in class. Often rephrasing the question gives the student an opportunity to think about it and give the correct answer. This should, however, not be overdone. If the student indicates he definitely is not going to answer the question, do not waste the class time by trying to elicit a response from him. If the student does not seem willing to answer a question or does not know the answer, the instructor should let another student answer this question.

(d) All answers should be recognized and evaluated.

The instructor will encourage correct answers if the student is given credit for the answer he has given. The instructor should evaluate the answer and point out the parts of the answer that are correct and correct any part of the answer which may have been given incorrectly.

  (e) Other students should be encouraged to comment on the question.

  To stimulate learning on the part of the student, other members of the class should be given an opportunity, if the situation permits, to evaluate the answer given by the student who answered a specific question.

We have discussed some of the procedures in asking and receiving answers to questions. Use of the questions can be very helpful in student learning. However, the instructor must know how to make the best use of questions and prepare in advance for the use of questions in his instruction.

Demonstration Method

  The demonstration method is the third general classification of methods in presenting material. The value of the demonstration method can be shown by simple tests. For example, try to tell another person, without using your hands, how to tie a tie. Or try to use words to tell a recruit how to make a complete search of a person who has been arrested.

  The demonstration method can be best defined as teaching by showing. Demonstrations should be used much more in teaching in the police school. Often we try to do by words what we could much more easily do by "showing" or demonstrating. The demonstration method is very seldom if ever used by itself. The demonstration must be generally used in conjunction with other methods. It must combine showing with telling. The purpose of the demonstration is to show how a skill, a procedure, or a process is performed so that the student will be aided in learning this skill or acquiring the knowledge necessary to learn the skill. A demonstration may be given to show the student *what* is done, *why* it is done or *how* to do it. Demonstrations either precede or follow the discussion. The demonstration method has advantages and disadvantages. Some of these will be discussed in the following paragraphs.

Advantages

  (1) *Makes explanations concrete for the students.*

For some sudents, mere telling may be just words as the students may not be able to visualize or understand the material being presented. A demonstration, however, gives meaning to these words and facts. For example, telling a recruit the facts and procedures to be followed in taking fingerprints will probably have very little meaning, while a simple demonstration of how a fingerprint can be used to solve a crime will have much more meaning and be much more concrete as far as the student is concerned.

(2) *Appeals to several senses.*

In the lecture and to some extent in the conference technique of instruction, the student only hears. When the demonstration is used, the student has an opportunity to actually see a thing being done and in some instances, may be able to actually touch the equipment. Much more learning takes place when more of the five senses are used by the students.

(3) *Have dramatic appeal.*

When well planned and well staged, a demonstration had a dramatic quality which not only arouses the classes' interest but intensifies learning.

(4) *Eliminates misunderstandings.*

Often explaining verbally how a thing is done leaves a student with a lack of understanding as to what actually takes place. A good demonstration not only eliminates misunderstanding but can be used to explain certain skills, techniques and procedures quickly and thoroughly.

(5) *Gives the students an over-all perspective.*

Students who see a demonstration see a complete performance of the procedure or complete development of the principle. They can see how each step is related to every other step and to the final accomplishment of the objective. They are made aware of what the objective actually is by seeing it attained.

Disadvantages

(1) *It is not practical for some subjects.*

Of course, the greatest disadvantage of the demonstration method is that it can not be used in teaching all types of subject matter. For example, in teaching such things as constitutional law, or history, it is not practical to use the demonstration method. The demonstration can be more efficiently used in teaching skills and techniques. In some "knowledge" subjects, the demonstration can not be used.

(2) *Require equipment and preparation.*

Demonstrations often require special and expensive equipment to make them effective. For example, in some instances, cutaways or models are required in order for the whole class to see the demonstration. The instructor must be well prepared and have made test demonstrations before he comes to class. Since the demonstration method is an effective way of teaching, the instructor should be furnished the equipment and time to prepare for this demonstration so that he can do it in an effective manner.

(3) *The size of the class is limited.*

For the demonstration to be effective, and for all of the students to closely watch the demonstration, the size of the class must be limited. This, to some extent, can be overcome by using large models for a larger class. When using the actual equipment, such as a demonstration of how the service revolver is used, the size of the class must be limited to the number that can actually see the demonstration.

Principles to be Followed in the Demonstration

(1) *Be sure the demonstration works.*

Before undertaking a demonstration in a class, the instructor should be sure that he can perform the demonstration, that he has the qualifications and that the equipment which is to be used, will work properly. Nothing falls as flat as a demonstration that does not work.

(2) *Prepare the students.*

Before conducting the demonstration, the instructor should be sure that the objective of the demonstration is known by the students. Explain the purpose and importance of the demonstration and the equipment. Tell the students what to look for.

(3) *Be sure that the students can see and hear.*

Seat or arrange the students so that they can see what the instructor is showing. The instructor should be sure that he stands so that he does not hide the equipment while explaining it. It is a good idea to show the actual equipment which will be used in the field even if a model is to be used.

(4) *Explain how it works and why it works.*

In conducting a demonstration, the instructor should be sure that he explains how the equipment works and what makes it work. This will give the students a better understanding of the equipment. The students can more readily understand a process if they can see a thing done and hear it explained as they see it.

(5) *Have the students participate.*

The instructor should ask questions of the students as he demonstrates and allow the students to ask questions. If possible, a member of the class should be allowed to demonstrate after the instructor has completed his demonstration.

(6) *Emphasize safety precautions.*

If the instructor is demonstrating a procedure that the students will have to duplicate, he must be sure that they know how to handle the equipment safely before they work with it. He should demonstrate how to handle the equipment safely and whenever possible, show the effects of mishandling and misuse. The example set by the instructor will be followed by the students.

(7) *Check and evaluate understanding.*

The instructor should use questions to determine if the students know the procedure to be followed and if they have learned the principles to be applied. The real test of their understanding will come in the next phase, the application phase. However, to some extent, the instructor can determine after the demonstration if the students have learned from the demonstration.

Use of the Demonstration in Police Training

One of the primary purposes of training in the police field is to teach the students skills and techniques. Often the use of demonstrations is overlooked in teaching in the police training school. In addition to using the actual equipment, the demonstration can be effective by using such things as motion pictures. These show the internal working of equipment which the students would only otherwise imagine. Also, skits can be used showing an incorrect and correct way of performance. Field demonstrations showing the students how to make an arrest or to stop a traffic violator are seldom used but should be used in the police training field.

Some of the areas where demonstrations can be used in the police training field are as follows:

(1) Making an Arrest, (2) Investigating at a crime scene, (3) Stopping a vehicle, (4) Searching a person after an arrest, (5) Making a Search of an automobile, (6) Firing a Weapon, (7) First Aid, (8) Disarming Tactics, (9) Investigating an Accident, etc.

Where the demonstration can be used to more adequately teach the subject matter, it should be used by the instructor even though it takes a little more time to prepare.

CLOSING

Summary

In this chapter, entitled "Methods of Presenting Instruction," we have discussed the three general methods of presenting instruction. These are the lecture method, the conference method and the demonstration method. We have learned that the instructor must consider the advantages and disadvantages of each method in determining how he will present his instruction. We have also considered the principles to be followed in the use of each of these three methods of instruction.

It is re-emphasized that it is often necessary and desirable to use a combination of methods in presenting material. However, the type of material, the time available, the size of the class and many other factors will determine which method or combination of methods the instructor can use to most efficiently develop student learning.

Closing Statement

Just as the doctor determines in advance the methods he will use in performing an operation, and the attorney determines the methods he will use in arguing his case, the instructor must determine in advance the method or methods he will use in guiding the students in learning. Just as the doctor must know the various methods available and the disadvantages and advantages of each, so the instructor must know the methods by which he can present his material and their advantages and disadvantages. To a great extent, the success of the instructor will be determined by his choice of methods.

Chapter 6

LEARNING BY APPLICATION

INTRODUCTION

Reasons for Chapter

In order for a police officer to learn to perform his duties, he must be told *what* he is to do, shown *how* to do them, and given an opportunity to *practice* them until he is able to perform satisfactorily. The officer is often called upon to learn a technique or a skill. The purpose of this chapter is to help the instructor in the police training school to develop the skill or technique on the part of the police officer by application; to help the student learn by *doing*.

Objectives of Chapter

In this chapter the application stage of instruction will be discussed. Included will be a discussion of principles to be applied by the instructor in conducting the practical exercise where the student is actually *doing* the thing being taught.

Review

We have now discussed the first stage in the teaching process; the planning stage, and the second stage, the presentation stage, where the student is told and shown. In this chapter we shall discuss the third stage; learning by application.

Procedure

In discussing the application process, we shall first discuss the place of application in the teaching process; secondly, opportunities for application in police training; thirdly, learning skills and techniques; fourthly, basic methods of application by the students; fifthly, techniques in performance; and sixthly, conducting the critique.

BODY

The Place of Application in the Teaching Process

It is difficult to imagine a person trying to learn to play golf or trying to learn to swim without actually practicing. Skills and techniques and to some extent, appreciations can only be learned or acquired by *performing* the activity. This is called the application stage of instruction or learning by doing. Application is combined with other stages of instruction. It may come anywhere in the lesson but normally it would come immediately after the explanation and demonstration. The application is also often combined with the examination to evaluate the student progress and to check the effectiveness of the instruction. Student activities or "doing" may occur in many forms. It may involve carefully chosen physical activities such as assembling a weapon or driving an automobile, or it may involve mental activities such as reasoning, understanding, and problem solving.

Opportunities for Application in Police Training

Too often in the police training school, the students are *told* what they should do but are not given an opportunity to actually practice. This results in many unnecessary mistakes being made by the men when they first go into the field. It is much better to avoid such mistakes by letting the students learn the techniques by practice. The instructor needs only to think seriously to find many areas where the student could learn by doing. Some of these are as follows:

  a. Making the physical arrest.
  b. Correct procedure in stopping an automobile.
  c. Pursuit driving.
  d. Lifting latent prints.
  e. Investigating a mock crime.
  f. Making a traffic accident investigation report.
  g. Interviewing.
  h. Conducting a surveillance.
  i. Radio and communications technique.
  j. Report writing.
  k. Testifying in Court.

These are only some of the areas in which the student will learn better by doing. Some others, of course, are firearms training, and armed and unarmed defense. The latter two mentioned are probably the only two that are being taught by the use of the application method in many police training schools. In the technical field, the instructor can also make good use of the application technique in learning.

Learning Skills and Techniques

Skills and techniques are not developed by merely telling the students how to do a thing or showing him how. Before any skill is learned, the student must be given an opportunity to do it and do it frequently. Of course, some skills are more difficult to learn than others and the time spent on practice will vary according to the skill or the technique to be learned. One educator has indicated that in teaching a skill or a technique, 10 percent of the time should be spent in explanation or in telling the student, 25 percent of the time in demonstrating the skill or technique, and 65 percent of the time in practice. In learning a skill the learner must:

a. *Gain a Concept of the Skill.*

The students first must gain an idea of the procedures to be followed in performing the skill or technique. The instructor gives the student this concept by telling him about the skill or technique and demonstrating how the skill or technique works. This concept of the skill can also be conveyed to the student by assigning definite reading material to be read comprehensively before trying to actually perform the skill.

b. *Develop the Skill.*

In this second phase, the student performs slowly as demonstrated by the instructor. In the Army we knew this as following the instructor's demonstrations, "by the numbers." In developing the skill, before actual practice, the student is required to perform each step of the procedure. He must, step by step, imitate the instructor.

c. *Practice for Accuracy and Speed.*

After the student has been given the concept of the skill, and has gone through the performance step by step, he is ready for practice. The amount of practice will depend upon the difficulty of the skill or technique. The practice should first be for accuracy generally, and then after accuracy is acquired, speed should be developed. The goal should be to make the skill or technique, to a great extent, automatic.

Basic Methods in Application by the Student

The success of the applicatory training depends upon the choice of the proper methods in the performance stage of instruction. The method to be used depends on the state of training and the skill to be learned. Some of the methods which can be applied are as follows:

a. *Group Performance.*

In the group performance method, all of the men in the class do the same thing at the same time and at the same rate under the supervision of the instructor or instructors. In this method, each of the students goes through the various phases or skills or techniques. The instructor first explains and demonstrates while the student observes. The student then goes through each step with the instructor and the instructor corrects any errors made by the students. A good example of this method is the disassembly and assembly of weapons. The instructor first shows the students how to assemble and disassemble the weapons, then each student goes through the procedure step by step until he has performed accurately. Most skills and techniques, and especially skills, can be taught initially by the group performance method. The number of phases that the instructor explains or demonstrates before the class will depend upon the nature of the subject and the ability of the students.

Because the group performance method affords maximum control by the instructor, it is ideally suited for the first two steps in learning a skill, that is, gaining the concept and perfecting the movement pattern. However, this method cannot make the skill automatic. To achieve this, a method which permits independent practice is required.

b. *Independent Practice.*

To acquire proficiency, the student may have to perform many times. Although he might have followed the instructor through the steps exactly, he may need practice to develop skill or dexterity. In some cases, the operation being of such a nature that it must be performed automatically, drill may be necessary. In the independent practice method, the student works at his own speed without control but with supervision. Constant evaluation by the student to see where his performance is weak and where his attention and practice must be concentrated is necessary. In learning a skill or technique by practice, the instructor must be sure that the student is practicing correctly. He must correct all errors which might lead to the formation of wrong habits or procedures.

c. *Coach-pupil Instruction.*

In many instances, a situation exists whereby the most effective performance can be gained through the coach-pupil method. A good example of a situation where this can be used is the learning of disarming techniques. The coach-pupil method may be used in several ways. First, the instructor could work with a student to develop the fine points of the skill. This type of instructor-student relationship is very concentrated since there is one student and one instructor. This type of instruction may also be used effectively with a large group. After the instructor has demonstrated a correct performance of an activity or procedure, he divides the students into teams of two members each. The members of each team then alternate in acting as coach and student. In this way, each student has an opportunity to practice the performance and to observe and evaluate someone else's performance. This method also develops initiative, reliance, and skill in giving directions and instructions.

d. *Problem Solving.*

Another method which should be considered by the instructor in developing techniques is the problem-solving method. After the student has learned certain skills and gained knowledge he can acquire confidence by solving problems. A good example of how this can be used is in the investigation of a mock crime. After the student has been taught the techniques of handling, preparing, and preserving evidence, a mock crime can be set up where he is given an opportunity to apply the skills and knowledge he has gained, thereby developing a technique. Here he is required not only to use the skills he has developed such as the lifting of prints and the proper handling of evidence but must apply all of these toward a successful solution.

We have discussed some of the methods to be used by the instructor in the developing of skills, techniques and appreciations in the application stage of instruction. The instructor who carefully evaluates these techniques or methods and uses ingenuity will do a much more effective job of instructing.

Techniques in Performance

The objective of the instructor in the application stage of instruction is to give the students an opportunity to apply directions, thereby learning skills and techniques and developing appreciation. If the instructor is to accomplish this effectively, there are a number of things he must keep in mind in guiding the student's performance.

a. *Plan for Student Performance.*

The instructor must *plan* the entire lesson. He must have a clear picture of the objectives to be attained, the procedures to be used, and the degree of attainment he expects. He must plan the explanation and demonstration which will precede the performance, make certain all materials and supplies are at hand, and be sure that all equipment to be used is in serviceable condition. The instructor should plan to make the situation as realistic as possible and use the actual equipment which will be used by the students on the job.

b. *Prepare the Student for Proper Performance.*

A student must be motivated to learn. The instructor cannot expect the student to see the need for this learning, therefore the instructor should demonstrate, explain, pose problems, and ask questions in the presentation to motivate the students. A student is further motivated if he understands each step of the procedure or skill before he goes to the next step.

c. *Guide the Performance.*

In this phase of instruction, the student is learning by doing. It is better for the instructor to let the student do the thing as much as is possible and give him only indirect assistance. The student must be trained to depend upon his own ability to solve problems. In guiding the performance of the student, the instructor should encourage questions from those who are having difficulty and be slow to reprimand. At the same time, however, the instructor must prevent the formation of faulty habits on the part of the students.

d. *Give Individual Attention.*

The instructor should observe each student's performance. He should help the student who needs help by giving him constructive criticism. The instructor can assist the individual in learning by asking questions of the student which will cause him to think. Have him consider hypothetical situations which he might encounter on the job. For example, in teaching the procedures of making a physical arrest, the instructor might say "what would you do if the arrestee started to run?"

e. *Evaluate the Performance.*

This evaluation of performance can be made by the student himself, by another student, or by the instructor.

When the student is able to analyze his own performance and to criticize it, he is aware of the objective. The student should be encouraged to constantly evaluate his performance in trying to make it conform to standards.

Another student can also be used to evaluate the performance of the student if this is done carefully.

The third method of evaluating performance is for the instructor to observe the student as he works, noting what he does right and what he does wrong. It is true that this type of evaluation takes much of the instructor's time, however the results will justify the use of the time by the instructor.

Conducting the Critique

Every practical exercise should always be followed by a critique. The purpose of the critique is to review the points covered, to point out the areas in which the students have done well and to correct any errors that have been made. Unless the critique is conducted after the practical exercise, the students may not have a clear, orderly idea of what has been done correctly and what has been done incorrectly. It is difficult to state exactly where the critique should come in the teaching process. Some writers feel that the critique should be the last stage of instruction and should follow every application period and every examination.

The instructor should use common sense in determining where the critique should be given. It should certainly follow every practical application so there will be no doubt in the student's mind as to what he did correctly and what he did incorrectly. In many instances, it should also follow the examination. If many of the students failed certain questions on the examination, the answers will probably never be made clear to the student unless there is a review or a critique following the examination.

The effectiveness of the critique depends upon the flexibility with which the instructor employs it.

a. *Uses of the Critique.*

(1) To give a complete picture of what has been taught. Often the subject matter has been practiced in parts. During the critique, the instructor can tie all of these parts together and clarify any phases which are not entirely understood.

(2) Indicate the strong and weak points of a performance. The students as individuals and the class as a group will have a more complete understanding of the skill or technique being taught if the strong points of the performance have been emphasized and the weak points discussed. The instructor should, of course, not only emphasize the weak points but the strong points as well.

(3) To re-emphasize the fundamental points of the lesson. Whether the critique follows the application or the examination, the instructor has another opportunity to point out or to emphasize the teaching points.

b. *Principles in Conducting the Critique.*

(1) Be considerate of the students. The student will gain very little if he is made angry or resentful. Therefore, the instructor should not be sarcastic and should make his criticisms or comments in a straight-forward personable manner. The strong points of the performance should be pointed out as well as the weak points.

(2) Be specific. In conducting the critique, the instructor should be specific in pointing out strong points and weak points. Generally saying that the performance was good, excellent or superior or to say that the performance was poor does not benefit the student. If the performance was not satisfactory, the instructor must point out exactly the specific areas in which the performance can be improved.

(3) Emphasize fundamentals. Where the critique follows the application, the instructor should emphasize fundamentals when possible. If there is more than one correct way of solving a problem, the instructor should not insist upon his method. He should evaluate and criticize the

various methods or solutions on the basis of their completeness and effectiveness and observance of the fundamental principles.

(4) Encourage student participation. A well controlled class discussion of the performance makes the student feel that he is a part of the critique and feels that this is a period set aside for learning rather than a period for criticism. On the other hand, the student should not be allowed to argue the answers when the critique follows the examination. If the instructor is not careful, the critique will develop into an argument whereby the student is given an opportunity to justify his answer rather than learning the correct answer.

(5) Make instruction foremost. It is often difficult to make the student, especially in advanced police training classes, understand that the critique is a period of learning. For this reason, the instructor must constantly be alert to keep the discussion on the subject matter and not let the students take over the initiative as to the points to be discussed.

CLOSING

Summary

In this chapter, we have discussed the application phase of instruction. This is the stage where the student learns by *doing* in developing skills and techniques. If he learns by doing in the training school before he is authorized to go into the field, fewer mistakes will be made in the field. We have discussed the areas in police training where the application phase of instruction can be used. Many police training schools fail to recognize the value of the application phase of instruction.

In this chapter, we have also pointed out that skills and techniques are mastered, not in the telling stage of instruction or the showing stage, but to a great extent in the doing stage or the application stage of instruction. In this application stage of instruction, there are basic methods which the instructor must consider in order to determine the best method to reach his objectives.

We also discussed in this chapter some of the techniques that should be followed by the instructor in performance. The final point that was discussed was the critique. The critique plays a very important part in the teaching process and should be used by the instructor to emphasize the teaching points and to give the students an overall view of the operation.

Closing Statement

In developing skills and techniques, and applying knowledge to problems, the student learns by doing. He either learns these skills and techniques and solves these problems in the training school or he learns these skills and techniques and solves these problems after he gets into the field. Waiting until he gets into the field could be too late.

Chapter 7

EVALUATION

INTRODUCTION

Reasons for Chapter

The instructor cannot assume that the student has learned the teaching points presented. The purpose of all educational endeavor is to promote student learning. The extent to which the student has mastered the desired skills and abilities or has changed his attitudes is the extent to which the instructor has succeeded or failed. The instructor then must determine by some means of evaluation, just how much learning has taken place, and if he has succeeded in guiding the student in learning.

Objectives of Chapter

In this chapter we shall discuss the various methods that the instructor may use in determining if the students have learned. We shall also discuss the characteristics of evaluation instruments and how to prepare an examination.

Review of Previous Instruction

In the previous chapters we have discussed the various phases of the teaching process. We have discussed the planning stage, the presentation stage, the demonstration stage, and the application stage. The learning process is not complete without an evaluation or testing stage of instruction.

Procedure

The chapter is divided into eight broad areas. We shall discuss them in the following order: 1) the evaluation objective, 2) Selecting the evaluation method, 3) Characteristics of the evaluation instruments, 4) How to prepare the written examination, 5) Preparing the performance evaluation, 6) Preparing the observation, 7) Administering the evaluation device, and 8) Interpreting test results.

BODY

Evaluation Objectives

Why are evaluation devices necessary? Why do we have examinations? Often the instructor thinks only of the written test when he thinks of evaluation or examination. However, there are many other types of evaluation devices and many reasons for giving examinations. Some evaluation devices are designed for some purposes, some for others. Among the purposes of tests or evaluation devices are the following:

To Determine if the Student has Achieved the Course Objectives

In some way the instructor must determine if he has achieved his objectives. The objectives, will, to a great extent, determine the type of examination or evaluation device that will be used by the instructor. The instructor should be able to state the objectives of the training course exactly, definitely, and simply. If the objective has been to teach the student to perform a skill or develop proficiency in a certain area, the test should be designed to determine if the student can do this. If the student is able to perform in a proficient manner, the instruction has been successful. If the objective of the teaching has been to develop knowledge on the part of the student, the test should be designed to determine if the student has acquired this knowledge.

To Improve Instruction

Another objective of the evaluation device or test is to determine how instruction can be improved. By studying the results of the evaluation devices, the instructor can determine the relative effectiveness of the various methods and techniques. If the instructor finds by his examination that he is not putting the teaching points across, it may be necessary to re-teach this class or use different methods in teaching the next class. This purpose of the examination is often overlooked by the instructor.

To Motivate the Students

When a student is made responsible for learning, he will learn more rapidly and pay attention in class. This could be called negative motivation. However, anyone who has been an instructor will soon find that the students will be more alert and learn more if they know an examination is to be given. There is, of course, a danger of over-emphasizing the examination results. A more positive means of motivation is preferable. Students who study or who pay attention merely to pass the examinations, often forget what they have learned.

To Provide a Basis for Assigning Grades

Some method must be used to determine which students have attained the minimum standard of performance and which have not. The various evaluation devices should be selected and used to determine if the students have attained the knowledge, skills, or techniques which are necessary in performing police work.

To Provide a Basis for Selection

No test is foolproof. However, in selecting men to perform various functions in the police service, some type of examination or evaluation device must be used. The various achievement tests and aptitude tests as well as the intelligence tests, furnish information for selection and guidance of personnel.

Selecting the Evaluation Method

As we pointed out in previous discussion, there are many reasons or purposes for the use of the written examination or other evaluation device. Each evaluation method has its advantages and limitations. The instructor must, therefore, be careful to choose the method which will most adequately achieve his purpose in evaluation. The general classifications of evaluation devices are as follows:

Written Examination

Generally, when we use the word "examination" or "test" we think of the written examination. However, the written examination is *not* the best examination in all instances. The written examination is good for measuring knowledge but only indirectly measures the student's ability to apply knowledge and skills. It cannot be relied upon to determine if the student has learned to perform a skill or technique. Under another heading in this chapter we shall discuss the various types of written examinations and how each can be used most profitably.

Performance Tests

The most reliable test, when it is practicable, is the performance test. It is just what it says, a test that is designed to measure how well a student can perform a given piece of work. If the subject matter being presented to the students is designed to teach the students a skill, the performance test is the best type of test. The evaluation of job proficiency is far more important than the evaluation of grasp of course content. The performance test is different from the observation technique in that the performance test is an exacting rate. For example, in giving a performance test to a student who is being taught to make the proper approach to stop a violator, certain definite and specific requirements should be included. If he does the thing he is supposed to do, he gets this checked, if not, he is marked off.

Some principles to consider in constructing the performance test will be considered under another heading in this chapter.

Observation Techniques

The observation technique is not properly called a test. However, many phases of student behavior cannot be measured by one of the tests mentioned. For example, it is difficult to determine if a student has learned the techniques of public speaking or teaching. The best way to grade or check the student under such circumstances, is by observation. In the observation evaluation the rating is not as exact as in the performance test. In other words, in the performance test, he either performs the act or doesn't perform. In the observation type of grading, the degree of proficiency is indicated.

Oral Tests

Oral questions by the instructor enable him to effectively spot-check on student learning. The "questions" should be used in most classes to determine if the students have learned the teaching points. We have discussed the use of questions in the teaching procedure in a previous chapter.

The instructor must select the evaluation device carefully. As indicated the device selected to determine if the student has learned the subject matter, will, to a great extent, be determined by the objectives of the course of instruction.

Characteristics of a Good Evaluation Device

To choose the evaluation device best suited to the purpose to be served, the instructor must have a command of the wide range of evaluation methods and techniques. The good instructor will use any form of evaluation which promises to determine if the student has learned the subject matter or which will help the student in learning. The instructor is not necessarily limited by the evaluation methods indicated here or any place else. The instructor must determine by evaluation, both the student's understanding of a certain subject and his ability to actually perform the operation. A combination of several types of tests may be used in achieving this purpose. Regardless of the methods of evaluation used by the instructor, there are certain characteristics which should be followed in any type of evaluation. Some of these are as follows.

The Evaluation Device Should Be Valid

For an examination to be valid, *it must measure what it is supposed to measure.* This is the most important feature of the test. For example, does a test on "Laws of Arrest" test the student's knowledge of these laws or does it test his ability to read the question? It is easy for the instructor to think he is evaluating one thing when in reality he is reflecting something entirely different, and thereby, often getting a completely false picture. The instructor should ask these questions in determining validity. Will this device really indicate what I want it to? Do the results indicate what I am trying to find out or something else?

The Evaluation Device Should be Reliable

Regardless of what type of evaluation is used, the test must reliably measure accurately and consistently what the student has learned. In other words, if the student has made a passing grade on the test, is the instructor certain he has learned the subject matter? If there is a chance of guessing, a test isn't reliable, nor is the test reliable if the student has cheated or the instructor has aided him in his answers. To be reliable directions must be clear and simple and the test must be of sufficient length to provide an adequate sampling.

The Device Must Differentiate

To get the desired spread in results, the evaluation device must select the better students from the poorer students. Some writers say that the test must be discriminatory. To make the test fit this requirement, some less difficult questions should be asked and some more difficult questions. Some questions should be on the subject matter actually covered in class and emphasized. Other questions should be on material which the students have been required to study but which may not have been emphasized too much in class. The instructor should be able to determine from this test how to rate the students in his class.

The Device Should be Comprehensive

A good evaluation device, whether it is a written test or some other form of evaluation device, should be comprehensive. This means that the test should include enough points to insure the instructor that he is getting the information he wants. All phases of instruction should be represented on the test. For example, if the test is given on the Laws of Arrest, some questions should be taken from "arrest without a warrant," some from "arrests with a warrant," etc. Do not take all of the questions from one phase of the instruction.

The Device Should be Understandable

To meet the test of validity and to be a true indication of what the student knows, the test must be understandable. The instructor should avoid "catchy" or "tricky" questions. He should make each question so clear that it truly means what it seems to mean. Each item should be phrased in simple enough terms for the lowest level of student in the class to understand. The instructor must check carefully for items which could possibly be misread or misunderstood.

Objectivity Must be Considered

Many instructors advocate that every test should be objective. The test should be as objective as possible, regardless of the type of evaluation used. However, it is not possible to make every test objective and still obtain the results desired. To be objective, the test must be one that can be graded by several persons with each person arriving at the same score. In other words, the personal judgment of the person scoring the test does not affect the score. An example of the objective type of test is the true-false test where, regardless of who grades the test, the same score will result.

There are some subjects which cannot be graded by a completely objective examination. For example, if the instructor desires to know if the student can organize material and apply knowledge and facts to situations, he cannot determine this with an objective test. In many instances, only subjective type tests can be used by the instructor. Even here, however, the principle of objectivity can be applied. Even in the essay type of test, the instructor can, before making out the test, determine the points that he expects the student to cover in his essay type of reply.

We have discussed some of the characteristics which must be considered by the instructor in constructing his evaluation devices. As indicated, the test should be valid, reliable, should differentiate, should be comprehensive, should be understandable, and as objective as possible. As a matter of fact, all evaluation devices meet these requirements to a degree. On the other hand, none of the evaluation devices completely meet the requirements. There is, for example, no such thing as a completely valid test or a completely invalid one. No test measures completely the material it is supposed to test or completely only the material covered in that subject. The test on the laws of arrest will, to some extent, test the student's ability to read. This is true even if the test is worded in the most understandable language. Each evaluation instrument will fall somewhere between the two extremes and in each category. The instructor, however, must understand these characteristics and make the evaluation devices apply these requirements as much as is possible.

Selecting and Preparing the Written Examination

If the instructor has determined that a written examination is the best evaluation device, he should then select the best written examination to achieve the objectives. Each type of written examination has its advantages and limitations. Each may prove better under a certain set of conditions. The instructor may decide to use more than one type of examination to evaluate how much the student has learned. Therefore, the instructor should familiarize himself with the various types of written examinations and select the ones which will serve him. Some types of examinations and their advantages and disadvantages will be discussed.

The Multiple Choice

The most experienced test administrators feel that multiple choice tests are used more extensively and in a wider variety of situations than any other type of written test. In the multiple choice type of examination, the student has a choice of two or more answers. It is often called, the best answer test.

The multiple-choice test consists of two parts. One is the stem which asks a question, states a problem, or takes the form of an incomplete statement.

The second part gives choices, alternatives, or possible answers, one of which is the correct answer. Some points which will assist the instructor in preparing a multiple choice test are as follows:

(1) The stem and all possible answers should be so clear that the student will not be confused and not be able to answer the questions even though he knows the correct answer.

(2) The stem should not, by its wording, suggest the proper choice. The stem, if it is part of an incomplete statement, should not suggest the answer by making only one choice a complete statement.

(3) Each item should be an independent problem and should not reveal the answer to another item.

(4) The problem should contain only material relevant to its solution. Adding a lot of words only confuses the student and does not test his knowledge.

(5) Trivial, impossible, or obviously wrong choices should not be included. The student should not be able to answer the questions by merely eliminating the obviously wrong ones.

(6) Clues to the correct answer should be avoided. If the student can answer the question by clues, this is not a good test. A test under these conditions would not be valid or reliable.

(7) When a negative item is used, the connective

word or phrase should be emphasized. Often a student will miss a question because he overlooked a negative item or a word that would change the meaning of the answer. For that reason, such words as "*not*" should be underscored.

(8) Words or phrases which are common to all alternatives should be placed in the stem.

(9) At least four alternatives should be used in each multiple-choice test item. If only two choices are used, the student has a good opportunity to make at least 50 percent by guessing.

(10) The correct choices to items should be distributed among the possible positions. For example, one position such as (1) or (4) should not be favored for the correct answer.

True-False Questions

A true-false test consists of a number of statements, each of which is either true of false. The student is required to indicate which statements are true and which are false by placing the prescribed symbol in a space or block provided. Some instructors like the use of symbols such as "T" and "F," others a plus or minus. Also, the student may be required to underscore a "T" or a "F" which are included on the examination paper. The advantage of the true-false question is that it is easy to grade and is strictly objective. However, a disadvantage is that it is very difficult to construct a good true-false test and very easy to construct a poor one. A second disadvantage of the true-false test is that it permits guessing and a student has a 50-50 chance of responding correctly. A third disadvantage is that it does not measure the student's ability to apply principles.

An example of the true-false question is as follows: "An amendment of the Federal Constitution which relates to Search and Seizure is the 5th Amendment." "T" or "F." This question actually tests the student's knowledge as he must know which amendment relates to Search and Seizure before he can correctly answer the question. However, as pointed out, the student could flip a coin and have a 50-50 chance of answering the question correctly. Also, it does not give the student an opportunity to apply the principles which were taught by the instructor.

Some of the points to be observed by the instructor in constructing a true-false examination are as follows:

(1) Use a sufficient number of items. If only a few true-false questions are used, it does not determine accurately and validly the knowledge of the student.

(2) Make the statements understandable. If the true-false statement is so long and complicated that the student loses the chain of thought, it will not adequately or accurately determine his knowledge.

(3) Be careful with the use of words which make the answer obvious. A person who has taken quite a number of true-false tests will be quick to recognize such words as "no," "never," "always," "should," "all," and "only."

(4) Avoid "catch questions." A catch question does not accurately determine the student's knowledge.

(5) Do not tip off the answer by the length of the question. If the true statements are consistently longer than the false statements, or vice-versa, the student will quickly recognize it and the test will not be valid.

(6) Give specific instructions. In the true-false test as in other tests, specific instructions must be given to the students in order to get usable results.

Completion Tests

In a completion test, the student is required to recall one or more words that have been omitted from the statement. The correct word or words, when placed in the proper blanks, complete the statement to make it true. These tests have the advantage of requiring the student to recall the correct answer rather than merely recognizing the answer when he sees it. It also has the advantage of entirely eliminating the possibility of guessing. Unlike the true-false question, however, the completion question is not entirely objective. The instructor might have one word in mind to complete the sentence while the student may use a different word which must be evaluated by the instructor to determine if the student actually has the knowledge. Also the completion test may not be scored by a machine. One instructor might give a different grade from another. An example of the completion type question is as follows:

"The Amendment to the United States Constitution which relates to search and seizure is the......Amendment." This eliminates the possibility of the student guessing as he must know which Amendment refers to or relates to search and seizure. Some suggestions to be followed in constructing a completion type question are as follows:

(1) Have only one blank in a sentence. It is often difficult for the student to get the meaning of the sentence if more blanks are left.

(2) There should be only one correct response for each blank. The instructor must attempt to word the sentence so that there can be but one possible response. If more than one response can be used, and be correct, the test is less objective.

(3) Have the blank at the middle or end of the sentence rather than at the beginning. It is difficult for the student to get the meaning of the sentence if the word omitted is at the beginning of the sentence.

Matching Tests

The matching test is constructed by putting one list of items in the left hand column and a list of related items in the right-hand column. The student then is required to indicate by marking in the appropriate space on the answer sheet, the number of the word or phrase in column two, or the right-hand column, that is most closely related in the meaning of the item of column one, or the left-hand column. The easiest example of this type of test is to list a number of States in the left-hand column and the number of capitols in a scrambled list in the right-hand column. The student is then required to match capitols with the States. These are in the nature of the multiple choice but are a little more involved.

The matching test has the advantage of eliminating guessing to a great extent and also has the advantage of being objective. Some points to be observed by the instructor in constructing matching items are as follows:

(1) Place the column containing the longer phrases in the left column. This makes the mechanics of selection easier for the student.

(2) Inform the student in the directions whether he is to use items in the right-hand column *more* than once or *only* once.

(3) Set up the test so that the complete matching exercise appears on one page. It is difficult for the student to turn a page and then go back to the preceding page in order to match the items.

(4) Use the first item in the exercise as an example and relate the example to the entire matching exercise.

(5) Construct the test so that the student can enter a "number" or a "letter" in the space provided, rather than writing out the descriptive titles or using complicated nomenclature. This will avoid giving the advantage to students who can write faster.

Essay Tests

In the essay test, the student is given a question or a series of questions to discuss, evaluate, analyze, summarize or criticize. One purpose of the essay test is to measure the student's ability to organize and express his thoughts. The essay test should be selected when the purpose of the instructor is to determine how well the student can organize his thoughts and apply principles in solving problems. The essay test is very difficult to prepare and, of course, lacks the objectivity of the other written tests that we have thusfar mentioned. However, none of the strictly objective tests that we have mentioned test the student's ability to apply principles and knowledge to the solution of problems. The essay type test is especially good in police schools for the higher administrative officers or supervisors.

The greatest disadvantage of the essay test is that it is not objective. Also it takes longer for the student to take the examination and only a relatively few teaching points can be included. The points to be observed by the instructor in the preparation and use of the essay test are as follows:

(1) Use the essay examination only for those functions for which it is best adapted. Actual knowledge is more easily and more accurately measured by other types of tests.

(2) Essay type problems should be clearly stated.

The students should know exactly what type of discussion is desired.

(3) Determine in advance definite specifications for marking. The essay type test can be made more objective if the instructor, in advance, lists the teaching points he expects the student to include in his discussion.

(4) Announce in advance the weight each item has in the final score. The student should know in advance how much each question will count in the final score.

(5) Tell the student in advance what is expected when he is taking the essay type test.

(6) Avoid having the solution to one problem based on the response to another. If items are linked in this way, the student may miss entire series of questions instead of merely one question in that series.

(7) Have more than one instructor grade the test, if possible. This will make the test more reliable and to some extent more objective.

(8) Use code numbers of student's names on the essay test. The instructor can make his grading more objective if he does not know to whom the test paper belongs. He should therefore, if possible, put only a number on the test paper and match the student's name with the number only after he has graded the papers.

Preparing the Performance Test

As we indicated when discussing the selection of evaluation methods, one of the best methods of evaluating is through performance. If the material to be evaluated is such that a performance test can be used, this is the most logical method of determining if the student has learned. This is especially true in testing the student in skills or techniques. A written test does not always tell the whole story of a student's progress.

One of the advantages of the performance type test or evaluation is that it reveals weaknesses which are difficult to discover in any other way. The performance test or performance evaluation is, however, limited in application. In some areas it is impossible to use the performance test or at least not practical to use it. It also has the disadvantage of requiring more instructors to evaluate the student. Since the instructor can only check one, two, or three students at a time, it will take quite a bit of time to evaluate an entire class.

A good example of the use of the performance test in the police training field is testing the ability of the police officer to fire a weapon. The student may be able to tell the instructor all about the weapon, how it is made and what makes it work, but until he is able to use the weapon, he has not completed his training.

There are several principles the instructor should remember in constructing a performance device.

    a. Select the teaching points which should be measured by the performance test. Merely watching the student do something is not a performance test. The instructor must know in advance exactly which points he should watch for in the performance.

    b. Make a performance check-list. In order to be as objective as possible in evaluating the performance of a student, the instructor must have a check list. This list should state specifically the steps the instructor expects the student to perform. For example, in the firing of a weapon, the check list might include such things as preparing the weapon for firing, the proper position for firing, observation of the safety rules, the time element, and success in hitting the target.

    c. Prepare a set of directions and instructions to be followed by the student. In order for the performance test to be of value, the instructor must let the students know the purpose of the test, exactly what the student is to do in the test and the major factors to be considered in the grading of the performance.

Preparing the Observation Evaluation

In the observation type of evaluation, the instructor evaluates rather than makes an exact measurement. It is not always possible or practical to evaluate the progress of the student by means of a written test or by means of the performance test. Determining if the student can fire a weapon is not difficult; he either performs or he doesn't. However, in determining if the student has the ability to perform according to certain broad principles, the student cannot be as readily evaluated by means of the ordinary measuring devices. For example, in teaching the student to become an instructor, it is not possible to determine definitely and accurately how well he instructs until he gets before the class and presents teaching points.

The differences then between the observation technique and the performance test is that in the observation technique, the student is evaluated by a graduated scale such as "Very Good," "Satisfactory," "Unsatisfactory," etc. In using the performance evaluation, the student either performed or he didn't perform.

The observation technique can be defined as a systematic analysis of the outcome of instruction. The observation technique should be used when it is not possible to give an exact rating on the student or it is not possible to determine if the student has achieved the teaching objectives by use of the written examination. The observation technique is much more difficult to administer and much less objective than the other types of evaluation devices. It is difficult for the instructor to give a completely objective grade since his personal bias or background will enter into the grading and he will have a tendency to grade the student on a specific trait rather than generally. Some of the principles that should be followed by the instructor in preparing and using the observation technique are as follows:

a. Select and define the points to be observed and evaluated. Each point that the instructor intends to observe and evaluate must be selected and defined in terms of student behavior so that there will be no misunderstandings or ambiguities.

b. Make the observation comprehensive. In making the observation comprehensive, the instructor must evaluate the student on the basis of many phases of the subject taught.

c. Observe accurately and impartially. An observer must be alert to all that is happening. He must avoid letting his opinions or biases influence his judgement.

d. Make an accurate record immediately. Unless the

record is made immediately, on a check list, the instructor will forget the good or bad points and tend to evaluate the student on only one or two points.

e. Combine the judgement of several observers when possible. Observation by several observers make the observation more objective.

f. Use a standard grading form. Unless the instructor uses a standard grading form, his observation of the differences will be unfair. The rating form should include all of the points to be observed and a breakdown of these points if possible.

Administering the Evaluation Device

A poorly administered test is worse than no test at all. If the test is not given correctly, the instructor will not know how much the student has learned and the student will obtain the wrong attitude about the importance of the subject matter. Good test administration consists of more than just giving the students the test questions, a piece of paper, an answer sheet, and a pencil. If the evaluation device is to meet the requirements that we have discussed in this chapter, the administration must be carefully thought out. A low score resulting from incorrect instruction or emotional upset is not a true indication of a student's ability nor is a high score resulting from cheating or improper help by the instructor an indication of the student's ability.

Some principles which should be followed by the instructor in administrating the test are the following:

Have All Testing Material Ready

All blanks, special directions, tools, scratch paper or any other material to be used on the test should be ready before the test starts. The instructor should arrive at the class well in advance of the time for the test to start and check to see that everything is in readiness.

Make the Instructions Clear and Definite

The instructions concerning the time, the type of help the students can secure, the material which is to be used and other information should be definite and clear. If questions are to be allowed from the students during the test, the instructor should advise the students exactly the procedures to be followed in asking these questions.

Have Good Testing Climate

In order for the student to do his best, the testing room should be well lighted and ventilated. The students should be in a pleasant frame of mind and all distractions should be avoided. The test should be started in a business-like manner and the instructor must maintain order, allowing no interruptions.

Interpreting Results

The true effectiveness of any evaluation device can be determined only by an analysis of the results obtained. The instructor wants to find from the test or evaluation device if the students have learned the subject matter and if the instruction has been effective. The instructor must then use the results of the test to separate the qualified students from those not qualified and to indicate the relative degree of learning each student has attained. Some of the principles which should be applied when interpreting the results of evaluation devices are as follows:

Interpret Results with Caution

No test is perfect. A student who makes a 100 percent on the written examination does not necessarily know all the material which has been taught. Nor does a "0" indicate that the student necessarily knows nothing. Poor grades may have been caused by ambiguities, poor selection of items or distractions in the test environment. They might have been caused by the emotional or physical condition of the student. It is, therefore, better to give more than one examination or more than one type of examination in evaluating the students' learning.

Evaluate the Test Items

A detailed item analysis may reveal several areas where the test can be improved. The instructor should go over each question to determine how many students missed this question, and if this is the multiple choice type question, what answer was given most frequently? Each item should have been chosen originally for a specific purpose and the instructor must have determined in advance if this was an item which he expected many of the students to miss. With this item analysis the instructor can make his future tests better. He can also use the item analysis to improve his instruction. This will reveal whether the test requirement is too easy, too difficult, or lacking in discrimination.

Establish Grading System Carefully

The instructor should be very cautious in establishing his grading system. Arbitrarily setting 70 percent as a passing grade means very little. The percentage score is not a true indication of what the class has learned because tests often vary in difficulty. Although setting a percentage score is the easiest way to grade, it is often not fair to the students. It is often more fair to consider the student's performance and the instructor's opinion as well as the test score.

If the instructor intends to grade on the curve system, he should very carefully prepare and make a thorough study of the testing techniques. The curve system has its disadvantage as it is assumed that some students will always fail. In some types of classes, the instructor cannot make this assumption.

The instructor should keep in mind that the purpose of tests is not only to give the student a grade. The best evaluation of the student is reached when the instructor considers the practical work and the ability of the student to apply knowledge as well as the actual test scores. The judgement of the instructor can and should play a part in the grading of the student. This should be based upon the knowledge of the student, the instruction presented and the standards desired. It is difficult, if not impossible, to establish a critical score based on a formula which is mathematically applied to the test results.

CLOSING

Summary

In this chapter we have discussed the stage of instruction dealing with the evaluation of the students. The instructor cannot assume that the student has learned. He must have some method of determining how much the student has obtained from the instruction. We have discussed the evaluation objectives, the principles which should be followed by the instructor in selecting the evaluation method and some of the characteristics of a good evaluation method, and some of the characteristics of a good evaluation device. We have also discussed the methods which will help the instructor in preparing the various types of examinations, including the true-false exam, the multiple choice exam, the completion examination, the matching test and the essay type examination. To have a valid examination and to truly evaluate what the student has learned, we have indicated that the test must be administered correctly and the correct principles must be followed in interpreting the results of the examination.

Closing Statement

No training program is complete without some type of evaluation device to determine if the student has learned and the instructor has taught. Testing then becomes one of the most important phases in the training program.

Chapter 8

INSTRUCTIONAL AIDS

INTRODUCTION

Reasons for Chapter

The instructor has the responsibility of conveying ideas to the students. The instructor who has the ability to select, construct, and use instructional aids effectively will be able to perform this responsibility more satisfactorily.

Objectives of Chapter

The purpose of this chapter is to acquaint the instructor with another tool which will aid him in presenting his subject matter in a more understandable manner. In this chapter we shall discuss the reasons for using aids, the characteristics of a good aid, some specific types of instructional aids that can be used in police instruction, some guides for selection of aids and some techniques to be applied by the instructor when using instructional aids.

Review of Previous Instruction

In previous chapters we have discussed the foundations for learning, some principles of learning, and the steps the instructor should keep in mind when preparing and presenting his material to the students. In this chapter concerning instructional aids, we continue to discuss methods that the instructor can use to more adequately present the teaching points to the students.

Procedure

The material in this chapter will be discussed under six main headings. The topics are (1) Definition of instructional aids; (2) Reasons for the use of instructional aids; (3) Characteristics of a good aid; (4) Specific aids which will assist the police instructor; (5) Guides for the selection of appropriate aids and (6) Techniques in the use of instructional aids.

BODY

Definition

An instructional aid is any material device that will aid the instructor in presenting his subject in a more understandable manner or that will assist the student in learning.

In spite of the fact that tests have shown that students do not learn as much from hearing as they do from seeing, most instructors still attempt to utilize the teaching time to the best advantage by talking. Instructional aids had not been used extensively until World War II. The Armed Services, realizing that students would learn more by seeing, spent many thousands of dollars in developing instructional aids. It was estimated that during World War II, the Armed Forces used six times the quantity of training aids as were created for use in civilian education in all earlier years. Since the war, not only have progressive educators developed instructional aids of various types but many manufacturers have developed machines and equipment, which when used properly by the instructor, will help the students learn.

In this chapter, we shall use the word "instructional aids" to include any equipment or device other than the instructor's voice which is used in helping the students learn.

Reasons for Using Training Aids

The instructor who has tried to use words alone in describing the proper method of handling traffic at an intersection soon recognizes the value of a blackboard or other training aid to assist him in his explanation. There are many advantages in using training aids in instruction. Some of these are as follows:

Stimulates Interest

One of the most important reasons for the instructor's use of instructional aids is to keep the interest of the students. We have indicated that learning is an active process. In order for the student to learn, he must not only hear and see what is being presented but his mind must be active. The instructor who does nothing but talk is working under a handicap as the students will soon lose interest. The instructor who uses ingenuity and initiative in constructing and using instructional aids will find it much less difficult to keep the attention of the students.

Saves Time

Instructional aids not only enable the student to learn more effectively but enable him to learn faster. Some subjects are very difficult if not impossible to put over to the students by the use of words. In many instances, one diagram on the board will save the instructor many minutes of time. By the adequate use of instructional aids, much time is saved in developing understanding.

Makes Use of More of the Five Senses

As we pointed out in an earlier chapter, the senses are the channels to the students' mind. Words often fade away and are often inadequate to convey delicate meanings, understandings, and appreciations to the minds of the students. By using instructional aids, the instructor is able to reach the minds of his students through more than one of the sense channels.

Makes it Easier for the Students to Learn

Often a picture or a training aid is more valuable than many words. It is much easier for a student to understand what a fingerprint pattern is if an enlarged fingerprint is shown by a chart or projector than it is if the instructor tries to tell the student about a fingerprint.

Enables the Student to Retain the Material Longer

Studies during World War II indicated that the uses of instructional aids in the Army resulted in approximately a 35 percent increase of student retention of information. It logically follows that since students use both hearing and seeing when aids are used, the interest is stimulated. This results in not only easier learning but in retaining the material longer.

Clarifies Subject Matter

All instructors have at times found it difficult to make teaching points clear by the use of words. If it is possible for the instructor to put these teaching points in front of the student by means of a chart or some type of projection, the subject matter is made clearer to the students.

Adds Emphasis

By the use of training aids, the instructor can indicate the teaching points he feels should be emphasized. This can be done by using charts, venetian blinds, or projections with the points to be emphasized clearly indicated. When the student sees the points written and emphasized, he will understand them better and remember them longer.

Provides Uniformity in Learning

Due to the fact that student backgrounds are different, the pictures they receive in their minds from words of the instructor differ from student to student. For example, one student who is told by the instructor how to make an arrest may get an entirely different picture than another student who receives the same instruction. A description of how the arrest should be made may be good as far as the instructor is concerned. However, if the instructor uses a demonstration or various types of aids to show how the arrest should be made, all of the students will get similar mental images which will correspond closely to the actual facts the instructor wants to get across.

Makes Transition Between Points Easier for the Instructor

Not only can training aids be used to assist the student in learning but they can be used to assist the instructor in teaching. For example, if the instructor has several points to be conveyed to the students, he finds it much easier to make the transition between points by enumerating the points of a chart, venetian blind or projection of some type.

Assists the Instructor in the Management of the Class

The instructor who uses ingenuity in preparing his instructional aids will find that they will help him in managing his class. For example, as the various points for discussion are indicated on an aid, the instructor can call upon the student to discuss the point and the student will have this point before him, making it unnecessary for the instructor to repeat the area of discussion.

These are only some of the advantages of using training aids. The instructor who uses initiative and imagination will find many, many ways in which he can use instructional aids to bring about understanding and appreciation on the part of the students.

Characteristics of a Good Instructional Aid

In selecting an instructional aid, the instructor should have a purpose for using the aid. It is difficult to indicate the characteristics of an aid as the instructor should not be limited in his thinking. However, there are some characteristics which should be kept in mind by the instructor when selecting and preparing instructional aids.

The Aid Should be Appropriate

The aid selected by the instructor should be selected to assist the instructor in presenting the teaching points. The instructor should not try to build his lesson around the aid but instead, determine the teaching points first and then develop the aids which will be appropriate in presenting these teaching points.

The Aid Should be Seen by the Whole Class

The instructional aid is of little value if it cannot be seen by all of the students. In determining the size of the aid and the size of wording on the aid, the instructor should consider the size of the class, where the aid will be used, and the distance from the students in the back of the class to the aid itself

The Aid Should be Neat and Accurate

Often the instructor is limited in the materials with which he has to make the instructional aids. He should, however, remember that the aid is for the purpose of presenting points to the students and should be attractive to the students. The wording should be accurate and consistent. Words must be spelled properly and lettering uniform. In other words, the instructor should be careful not to use small letters in some places and large lettering in others. It is probably better to use capital letters on the aids that are hand-printed.

The Aid Should be Simple

The aid should not be cluttered up with unnecessary material as the student will soon lose interest in trying to figure out what the aid indicates. It is generally advisable to include only a few specific points on the aids so that the students will not become confused.

The Aid Should Emphasize Specific Points

Since the purpose of the aid, generally, is to emphasize teaching points, the instructor should keep this in mind in preparing these aids. Often underlining or color can be used to emphasize the points the instructor feels are important.

The Aids Should be Easy to Use

The aid should be selected for the person who is to use it. It is very distracting for an instructor to try to use an aid with which he is not familiar. It defeats the purpose of the aid if the aid is so complicated and so difficult to use that the instructor finds it time-consuming to get the aid in position and to explain the aid to the class. ·

The Aid Should be Portable and Durable

Generally speaking, aids will not be used for one class period only, but will be used over and over again. They should, therefore, be made by the instructor, keeping in mind that they must be stored and be of such construction that they will last long periods of time. Of course, there might be exceptions to this. Some situations might justify making aids for one particular class after which they will be destroyed.

The above characteristics of a good training aid are, as pointed out, merely suggestions for the instructor to keep in mind. Often, high police administrators will hesitate in approving funds for training aids. This makes it necessary for the instructor to make his own training aids using the material he can obtain at little cost. Even here, the instructor can use aids effectively. It should be pointed out to the administrator, however, that good instructional aids, even if they are more expensive than the administrator would like for them to be, are worth many times their cost in terms of saving the time of the instructor and the students. A thorough knowledge of the aids available and careful planning by the instructor will, to a great extent, reduce the cost of instructional aids to the very minimum.

While aids make learning easier for the students, they do not make the job of the instructor less difficult. In fact, if the instructor conscientiously selects his training aids, this preparation will take longer and will be more difficult. To perform adequately, the instructor must have plenty of time to prepare his lesson and his instructional aids. The students spend many working hours in class. This is not justified if the training is not the very best.

Specific Instructional Aids and Their Use

There are many types of instructional aids which can be used by the police instructor. Each aid has advantages and limitations and therefore should be carefully studied before a selection is made. The instructor should constantly examine the subject matter he is teaching in order to develop additional aids or different aids which will assist the student in learning. The various types of aids listed below are defined with some of the uses of these specific aids. In some instances, there are included some suggestions as to how the aids can be used most effectively.

Blackboard or Chalkboard

The instructional aid which has been used most commonly is the blackboard or more properly called, the chalkboard. Most classrooms are equipped with a blackboard or portable blackboards are available. No further definition of the blackboard is necessary here as this is a standard piece of equipment and can be purchased without difficulty.

    (1) *Suggested Uses of the Blackboard.*

        (a) *To designate teaching points.*

        One of the most simple methods of keeping the students advised as to what teaching points are being discussed is to designate these teaching points on the blackboard. This can be done as the instructor progresses or the points can be designated in advance and covered with strips of paper and pulled off as the points are covered.

        (b) *For diagrams and layouts.*

        The blackboard has great value in developing relationships and showing organization. The instructor who plans in advance can plan diagrams for use on the blackboard and can prepare layouts which help the student in learning.

        (c) *To emphasize important points.*

        The instructor, even though using primarily the lecture method of instruction, can emphasize important points by writing these points on the blackboard as his lesson progresses.

        (d) *To clarify students' questions.*

        The blackboard has the advantage over some types of aids as the instructor does not necessarily have to prepare as thoroughly in advance. If the student does not understand some points, the instructor can clarify this by spelling out a word, by writing the teaching points or by drawing a diagram to emphasize the point being presented.

These are only some of the uses of the blackboard. A good instructor will find many opportunities to make very valuable use of the blackboard.

(2) *Techniques in Using the Blackboard.*

The following techniques will assist the instructor in making the most profitable use of the blackboard.

(a) *Plan in advance.*

The lesson plan which has been prepared by the instructor should have layouts as to the material which will be placed on the blackboard. If the blackboard will not be used before the particular instructor uses it, he should put some of his material on the blackboard before the class starts. This will save the time of the students and the instructors. Often the instructor finds it attracts the attention of the students more if the blackboard work is done as the discussion progresses. The instructor can often impress the class as well as put over his points by the use of a pencil to lay out his work on the blackboard before the class starts. After the class starts the instructor can complete this by taking a piece of chalk and going over the pencil marks as the lesson progresses.

(b) *Check the equipment.*

Before the class starts, the instructor should be sure that he has enough chalk, erasers, ruler and other items to be used. He should also check the lighting on the board to determine if there is too much glare and above all, should be sure that the blackboard is clean and free of other material.

(c) *Make the wording and drawings large enough and bright enough to be seen.*

When using the blackboard, the instructor cannot afford to be a "space-miser" or a "secret agent." He must make the lettering large enough for the person in the back of the room to see. He must write in a strong enough hand that the students can see the writing or diagrams. He should not crowd the work together as this makes it impossible for the students in the back of the room to understand what he is trying to put across.

(d) *Keep the material simple and brief.*

Concise statements are most effective. One word with an oral explanation by the instructor will often serve to make the point clear.

(e) *Use color for emphasis.*

Often colored chalk can be used to emphasize certain points.

(f) *Erase unrelated material.*

Unrelated material on the blackboard distracts from the material which they should be looking at. It should be erased as soon as the instructor has finished using it.

(g) *Keep work neat, clean and orderly.*

The use of the blackboard will be more effective if the instructor keeps his work neat, keeps the blackboard clean and has his work on the blackboard organized.

Other techniques which can be applied to blackboard work as well as to other instructional aids will be included under another heading and should be referred to.

Overhead Projector

The overhead projector is one of the most versatile and easy to use projectors available to the instructor. This projector projects images from a transparent sheet to flat wall surfaces or to a screen. It projects many types of slides and in addition, enables the operator to write or draw and have the image of what he is writing or drawing projected on the screne at the time he is writing. This allows the operator or instructor to face the audience while presenting his material.

The overhead projector can be used to project silhouettes, opaque objects, transparent models to show actions of various devices, as well as printed material on the slides. Very dramatic effects can be obtained with the use of working models made of colored transparent plastic.

Several firms manufacture the overhead projector and will gladly furnish police instructors with all of the material concerning the projector, how it should be set up, and the cost. Some of the types of overhead projectors and firms which sell them are listed below.

Visual Cast, Victor Lite Industries, Inc.
4117 West Jefferson Boulevard, Los Angeles, California

Vu-Graph, Beseler Co., 219 So. 18th Street
East Orange, New Jersey

Transpaque Projector, Technifax Corporation
Holyoke, Massachusetts.

Most of these firms have representatives in the larger cities and will send representatives to the departments that are interested. Transparencies can be made for use on the projectors with little cost. The companies which produce the projectors also manufacture plastic sheets of various thicknesses and sizes which can be used for making the transparencies. Transparencies can be made for a single using or can be made and stored for use in the future. The instructor can make these aids himself by merely writing on the transparency material with india ink or with felt markers which include color or with a grease pencil. Most cities also have agencies now which will make transparencies at the request of business or, of course, for police departments.

One of the easiest ways to make transparencies is to write the material to be presented on a plain white sheet of paper and make positive or negative transparencies with the Thermo-fax copying machine. This method of making transparencies has recently been developed by the Thermo-fax Company. The manufacturer will send information concerning the machine and the materials available.

The Charles Beseler Company, the address which was included on the preceding page, also has a unit which will make transparencies. Any of the companies which manufacture the overhead projector will forward information on how to make transparencies for the machine as well as tips on how to make effective use of the overhead projector in teaching.

(1) Suggested Uses of Overhead Projector.

As pointed out, the overhead projector will assist the instructor in imparting ideas to the students in a clear and connected manner, will help to arouse their interest and stimulate them to develop and express their own thoughts. The instructor should use his imagination in the use of the overhead projector, and make use of the overhead projector when it will assist him in instructing. Some of the suggested uses of the overhead projector are listed. Many other uses can be made of this projector if the instructor uses ingenuity, and plans his instruction well.

(a) Project diagrams and illustrations.

Diagrams and illustrations will clarify and emphasize the meaning of the spoken word. For example, an organizational chart can be drawn up in advance and used on the overhead projector to show the organization of the police department. Diagrams showing crime scenes, traffic situations and many others can be used in training in the police department.

(b) Emphasize teaching points.

Even in subjects where it is not practical to draw a diagram, the teaching points which have been selected by the instructor can be taught more clearly if conveyed to the students by the use of the overhead projector.

(c) Project working models.

The overhead projector can be used very effectively to show how a piece of equipment works by making transparent parts of a working model. These can be placed on the projector and projected on the screen so all of the students can see the various parts.

(d) Project silhouettes.

The class can be shown how a thing looks by placing it on the projector so that the silhouette is projected on the screen.

(e) Project color and content of fluids.

To show the physical or chemical reactions of fluids, a small amount of the fluids can be placed on the overhead projector in a glass dish and the changes indicated on the screen when other fluids are added.

(f) Project material on blackboard.

It is possible to project an image on the blackboard from a slide that has been made up in advance and to complete the instruction by adding points with chalk on the board itself.

(g) Stethoscopic training.

An attachment can be placed on the overhead projector for use in teaching flash recognition.

(h) Project photographs.

By a special process, photographs can be made into transparencies and projected by the overhead projector onto a screen. Also, pictures and diagrams can be taken from books and projected on the screen.

(i) Show movement.

With the addition of a polarized unit, the overhead projector can be used to show movement. For example, the overhead projector with a polarized attachment can be used to show how the blood flows through the body.

These uses of the opaque projector are only some of the uses which can be made of the projector. The instructor will develop other uses as he becomes acquainted with the overhead projector and how to make transparencies for use on the projector.

(2) Techniques in using the overhead projector.

(a) Be familiar with the projector and how it operates.

(b) Plan the aids carefully before they are made.

(c) Place the projector and screen for best audience visibility.

(d) Use overlays when presenting detailed drawings or illustrations. This is done by taking more than one sheet of the plastic material and putting parts of the diagram or illustration on each of the overlays, thereby adding parts as the discussion develops.

(e) Practice using the projector to avoid distractions in the class. It takes practice to use the projector smoothly so as not to annoy the class.

Venetian Blind

The venetian blind is an upright frame containing a series of horizontal revolving slats. It provides a convenient means of displaying, item by item, the main points of the lesson, procedural steps and related principles or any list of teaching points. The venetian blind can be made in varying sizes to fit the needs of the class and the classroom. It can be made to slide back and forth as a sliding blackboard or can be made upon a frame.

Strips of white paper are inserted into the slats of the venetian blind so that they will fit into the retaining groves. If there are no retaining groves, the strips can be tacked on or taped to the slats. Also, the slats can be painted with blackboard paint which will enable the instructor to print with chalk directly on the surface of the slat. The advantage of the venetian blind is that one point can be discussed by the instructor at a time and the other points not be placed in view of the students until the instructor desires to consider them.

Hook N' Loop Board

The hook & loop board is made by covering a regular sized bulletin board with a cloth which has countless tiny nylon loops. By applying nylon hook tape to the back of various objects, they can be quickly placed on the board and will stay there securely until removed by the instructor. The instructor using imagination with the hook & loop board can make displays and visual aids which will assist the student in learning.

Slide Projectors

The 35mm slide projector can be purchased from any camera store as well as a 3¼" x 4" slide projector. These projectors can be used to project slides on the screen and be adapted to many uses by the instructor. A 35 mm slide projector can also use film strips which are often available at public libraries. A film strip is a series of single pictures on a continuous strip of film. The lantern slides are 3¼″ x 4″ slides. They can be made up several ways by the instructor. The regular polaroid camera has an attachment whereby this type of slide can be made with the camera and projected on the screen.

The use of the slide projectors to aid in teaching has many advantages. In a few minutes, a point can be put over to the class which would take many words to do. Slides arouse interest and attract attention and generally are not to difficult to prepare as well as not being expensive. A disadvantage of using a slide projector is that it must be used in a dark room and generally must be used from the back of the room, necessitating the instructor to leave his place in front of the classroom.

Opaque Projector

An opaque projector will project any printed material from the printed page to a screen. It will project material from text books, manuals, photographs, etc., without making these into transparencies. The instructor merely has to place the illustrated or printed material into position at the bottom of the projector, turn on the projector lights and the image is projected on the screen or wall.

The advantages of the opaque projector is that it will project color, will project from text books and other printed material, will project in picture form, objects such as a weapon and is easy to operate. A disadvantage of the opaque projector is that it must be used in a dark room, has some motor noise and requires the instructor to work in the dark and be away from the front of the classroom.

Motion Picture Projector

Many companies manufacture the 16mm motion picture projector. The training film or motion picture is very effective in arrousing the emotions and changing attitudes of the student. It can make the training more realistic by bringing actual events right into the classroom so that the students can see what is happening. They are valuable, in that they teach faster and more fully and can reach many students of different backgrounds. Also, points presented in the training film are usually remembered longer, especially if they are dramatized.

There are disadvantages to using the training film, however, of which the instructor or the supervisor of the instruction in a training school must be aware. First, training films are not available in all subjects. Many instructors will, however, still try to use a training film rather than prepare a lesson to present the teaching points that should be presented in this class. Too often, the instructor will consider the training film as an easy way to teach and not prepare for the class presentation.

(1) Techniques in Using Motion Pictures.

An advantage will accure to the instructor who uses motion pictures only if he uses them properly. Some points to be remembered in using motion pictures are as follows:

(a) Preview the film.

Unless the instructor has carefully previewed the film, he will not be able to determine if the key points in the film are those he wants emphasized in the lesson. He should plan in advance the necessary instructions and follow up activities which he will use.

(b) Check the equipment.

The instructor should be sure that the equipment is in good working order before the class starts. He should be familiar with the equipment in order to make emergency repairs in the class if trouble developes.

(c) Prepare the class for the film.

The instructor should prepare for the film by telling what the film is about, the important points to observe, and the relation of the film to earlier training. There is a difference between merely showing films and using them effectively as aids in instruction.

(d) Stop film to emphasize points.

Maximum use can be made of the film by the instructor's stopping the film to emphasize the teaching points as they occur. The Los Angeles Police Department has made very good use of this technique by filming supervisory situations and letting the students discuss the situation before reaching conclusions as to what action should be taken.

(e) Follow up with discussion.

To make effective use of a training film, the instructor should follow up the film with a discussion, practical application or a short test or a review of the points discussed. This type of activity will help "drive home" the lesson which the film is designed to teach.

(2) Using sound tract attachment.

The police instructor can make use of the magnetic sound tract with the 16mm film. This makes it possible for the instructor to record in advance the discussion of the film. It is especially valuable in teaching recruits what actions should be taken in specific situations which they will encounter in the field.

Sound Recordings

The instructor can make use of sound recordings in making his instruction more interesting and effective. By using the wire recorders, the tape recorder or records, the instructor can bring actual events before the class. For example, an entire recording of an actual interrogation of a suspect would help the student to understand interrogation techniques. Also, the recorder can be used in speech instruction classes, etc., in order for the student to actually evaluate himself.

As in other types of training aids, the instructor must thoroughly prepare before using the recordings. He should listen to the recording at least twice before using it and use the recording for a purpose, not just to fill in time. The recording must usually be accompanied by class discussion and be introduced properly in order to be effective.

Flip Charts

A flip chart is a series of charts fastened together and containing a series of diagrams or teaching points which the instructor wants to convey to the students. A flip chart or graphic training aid is very effective as it allows the instructor to present one idea at a time and then turn to the next chart for a second idea or teaching point. Several commercial firms now make flip charts with the frame to mount the flip chart on. If the frame is not available from a commercial concern, it can easily be made by constructing a simple "A" frame.

Some points to be followed by the instructor using the flip chart will aid in his use of this training aid. He should use short, crisp phrases; use large simple lettering, not crowd the message, eliminate fancy effects and use appropriate cartoons where practical.

Magnetic Board

Another effective training aid that can be used by the police instructor is the magnetic board. This type of board can be purchased commercially or can be made by using a properly galvanized iron sheet. To this, magnets can be attached to various types of charts, pictures, diagrams, etc., and placed upon the board. This type of board is especially good for teaching a student to investigate traffic accidents, to learn procedures in controlling traffic, etc.

3-dimension Mock-up

The Armed Forces have effectively used the 3-dimensional mock-ups to give the students an idea of what a scene actually looks like. This can be in the form of actual miniature screnes or by using sand boxes, cut-aways, relief maps, etc.

The disadvantage is that often these are expensive to construct, and unless the class is properly positioned, the mock-ups cannot be seen by all of a large class. If effectively planned and used properly, however, these are very effective teaching aids.

The specific types of aids indicated above are only some of the training aids which the instructor can use. Under our definition of training aids, many other devices can be used to help the student learn. The actual equipment to be used in the field is one of the best training aids. Others which are commonly used are charts, such as organizational charts, graphs, diagrams, maps made on large sheets of paper, large posters, bulletin boards, written instructional material, etc. Another type of training aid which is considered in a somewhat different category is the use of the field trip. If time permits, the field trip, whereby the student can actually visit and view a situation is more meaningful than any picture or a diagram which can be brought into the classroom.

Guides for Selecting the Appropriate Aid
Select an Aid Which will Supplement Specific Instruction

Do not select the aid, and then build the instruction around the aid. It is often tempting for the instructor to find an aid that is available and then build his lecture around the aid. The aid should be prepared or selected after the instructor has determined the teaching points he desires to convey to this class.

Select Aid or Aids Which are Usable

The instructor should be careful that he selects aids which can be used in the particular teaching situation. If the classroom is small, it will not be possible to use some types of teaching aids as they will distract more than add to the learning.

Select an Aid Which is Worth What It Costs

If an aid is not available and the instructor is to make an aid, he should select one that is not too expensive, considering the purpose and amount of use it will receive.

Select an Aid Which is Suitable to the Subject Matter

The instructor should carefully examine all types of training aids which are available and then select one which is suitable to this particular subject matter. For example, if the instructor is teaching a speech course, the sound recording would probably be more adaptable for use than some of the projectors.

Techniques in Using Instructional Aids

Even though the instructor knows the characteristics of a good aid, the types of aids that are available, and has selected the aid carefully, he will not be able to use the aid to maximum benefit unless he uses the aid correctly. Some techniques to be followed by the instructor in using the aid are as follows:

Prepare for Use of the Aid

The instructor should practice making use of the aid in advance. It is embarrassing to find that an aid will not work after the class has started. The instructor should have the aids numbered or in some way arranged so that he will be sure to use the correct aid at the correct time. Also his lesson plan which has been prepared in advance should have a notation as to when each aid will be used.

Explain How the Aid will be Used, If Necessary

If the aid is complicated or is difficult to understand by the students, the instructor should explain how the aid will be used and for what purpose. The aids will not do the teaching. Aids are to help the instructor, not to replace the instructor in achieving student development.

Keep Out of Sight When Not in Use

The aid should be covered or kept out of sight until the instructor uses the aid. This is not difficult on many types of aids. However, some, such as large charts and maps, should be covered or folded up when not in use. The aids will distract from the explanation being given if left uncovered or left where the student can see them.

Display Instructional Aids So They Can be Seen by all Students

If the aid is to accomplish its purpose, it must be seen by students in the rear as well as those in the front of the class. The finest aid is of no value if it cannot be seen.

Discontinue Discussion While Displaying the Aid

When pulling out a slide or making noises in displaying an aid, the instructor should discontinue his discussion. The students will miss part of the discussion if the instructor attempts to talk while preparing an aid for use.

Talk to the Class, Not to the Aid

The instructor should not become so involved in the training aid as to completely forget the students. If it is necessary to write something on the board, or work on an aid, the instructor should do this and then turn and discuss the material with the class.

Take a Position Which Will Not Obstruct the Students View

The instructor should not stand in front of the aid or put it behind the lectern. It should be in the position where all the students can see it. If a pointer is used, the instructor should stand to one side of the aid and hold the pointer in the hand nearest the aid so that he will not be facing the aid. After the pointer has been used, it should be placed on the desk or table so that it will not distract the class.

Display Aids Smoothly

The instructor should try not to use too many different types of aids. If he does, he will be spending much of his time changing from one aid to another. The instructor should practice using his aids so that he will not unduly disturb the class. The instructor should also be careful not to make a great deal of noise in taking down charts, "wadding" paper, etc., when using his aids; this only takes the attention of the class from the subject matter.

Remove the Aid When the Purpose has been Accomplished

After the aid has been used, the instructor should turn off the projector, if a projector is used, and cover other aids if it is not possible to remove them.

CLOSING

Summary

In this chapter, we have discussed the definition of instructional aids; have emphasized the purposes of instructional aids as tools for the instructor; have discussed the characteristics of a good instructional aid; and have indicated some specific aids which will be of value to the police instructor in helping the students learn. We have also discussed some of the guides which will aid the police instructor in selecting the appropriate aid for the occasion and have discussed some of the techniques the instructor can apply in using the instructional aids as teaching tools.

Closing Statements

Instructional aids are very effective tools in assisting the instructor to accomplish the objective of instruction, that is, aiding the student in learning. How well these tools serve the instructor depends upon his knowledge of their possibilities and how skillfully he uses them.

Chapter 9

MAKING THE LESSON PLAN

INTRODUCTION

Reasons for Chapter

After the instructor has completed his study and research, he will have copious notes which he must put in usable form. Study, research, and rough notes will be of little value to him unless he has the material organized for class use. If the material has not been organized into a lesson plan the instruction will be hap-hazard and disconnected. There is no surer road to teaching success than a carefully thought out lesson plan.

Objectives of Chapter

The purpose of this chapter is to emphasize the value of the lesson plan and to give the instructor some assistance in making out the lesson plan.

Review of Previous Instruction

In Chapter I, we discussed the various stages in the development process. We pointed out that the first stage in the development process is the *preparation* by the instructor. In Chapter III, we discussed the various steps that should be followed by the instructor in planning his lesson. One of these steps is making the lesson plan. We said that the lesson plan would be made only after careful analysis of the subject, careful review, and after the instructor had decided on the teaching points to be presented in the particular class.

Procedure

The material in this chapter shall be discussed in the following order:

a. Purposes of the Lesson Plan   d. Making the Lesson Plan
b. Types of Lesson Plans   e. Using the Lesson Plan
c. The Lesson Plan Form   f. Some Sample Lesson Plans

BODY

The Purposes of the Lesson Plan

Many instructors argue that a lesson plan is not necessary. They say "We have completed our research and we want to be free to do what we think best as the lesson develops." It is true that the instructor should be free within reasonable limits to modify his instruction to fit the special needs of a particular class. This, however, is no rationalization for not having a lesson plan. The lesson plan is not intended to cramp the style of the instructor but to make sure that the student receives the instruction necessary in this specific topic. Some of the more obvious purposes of the lesson plan are as follows:

Coverage

How can the instructor make certain that he has covered the material a student must know? The instructor must have spent much time in analyzing the subject to determine which teaching points should be presented. With the lesson plan he can be sure that his planning will be carried out and the students will be given all the teaching points.

Sequence

Also, in his planning the instructor has to determine the proper sequence in presenting the teaching points. With the lesson plan, he can be certain that the teaching points can be presented in this sequence; that is, they will be presented by proceeding from the simple to the complex.

Time Control

Have you ever been in a class where the instructor in his alloted time, completed only one half the material? If he had a lesson plan and had rehearsed the lesson, this would not have happened. If the student does not learn the teaching points the instructor feels are necessary in his class, he will probably never learn these teaching points. The instructor then must have some way of controlling the time he has allotted to him. This can best be done by the properly prepared lesson plan.

Confidence in the Instructor

The instructor who has a carefully prepared lesson plan is

confident that he can teach the material and that he will cover all the material well. This does not mean that he will read verbatim from the lesson plan but he knows he has the lesson plan there and can refer to it if necessary. This is especially true of the beginning instructor or the instructor who teaches only occasionally. There is no better way to control nervousness than by having a lesson plan.

Method

The instructor who carefully prepared his lesson will have planned for the use of training aids at certain points, the use of questions at certain points and the use of the review at other points. With the lesson plan, he can be sure that his method of teaching will be carried out. In briefly referring to the lesson plan, he can see that a training aid will be used at a specific point in the lesson. Without this reference to the lesson plan, some time might be wasted.

Record for Examination

How often have you complained in taking an examination that the material was not covered in class? The instructor who uses the lesson plan will not have this difficulty. When he is preparing his examination he can be assured that the material has been covered. There is no surer way of losing rapport with the class than by giving examinations on material that has not been covered in class.

Refresh Memory of the Instructor

Few men are gifted with such phenomenal memory that they need not refresh themselves on the material to be covered. Often a lapse of several months occurs from one presentation to the next. The instructor who has carefully planned his lesson need only to review his lesson plan, and refresh his memory on the material that is to be covered. The instructor should always review his lesson plan before presentation in order to eliminate unnecessary pauses and keep the lesson moving along effectively.

These are some of the purposes for having a lesson plan. The experienced instructor will find that the time spent on making a complete lesson plan is more than justified.

Types of Lesson Plans

There are many types and forms of lesson plans. Each has its advantages and disadvantages. The instructor should be familiar with the various types of lesson plans in order to choose the plan that will best accomplish his purpose.

Topic and Sentence Outline

Actually the *topic* outline and the *sentence* outline are two different types of lesson plans. We are considering them together here, as the advantages and disadvantages of these two are practically the same. In a topic outline, the main points and subpoints are noted in brief phrases or single words. For example, a topic outline to be used in the laws of arrest would read as follows:

"I. Arrest Under the Authority of a Warrant.
    A. Constitutional Provisions of Fourth Amendment and State Constitutions.
    B. Persons Empowered to Issue Warrants.
    C. Grounds for Issuing Warrants.
    D. Form and Content of Warrants."

In the above illustration, only the topics are given.

The sentence outline differs from the topic outline in that each point is a complete sentence rather than just a word or a phrase. For example, in the lesson plan for laws of arrest, the sentence outline would be as follows:

"I. Arrest Under the Authority of a Warrant.
    A. The provisions of the fourth amendment of the U. S. Constitution state constitutional provisions limit the circumstances under which a warrant can be issued.
    B. Only certain persons have powers to issue a warrant.
    C. There are specific grounds which must be complied with before a warrant can be issued.
    D. The form and content of warrants vary from state to state."

(1) *The Advantages of a Topic or Sentence Outline:*
    (a) Reminds the instructor of the points to be covered. The topic or sentence outline is often sufficient to remind the instructor of the points he wants to cover

under a certain heading. Since the topic or sentence outline contains none of the real discussion to be presented to the class, it, of course, does not help the instructor in this way.

(b) Guide for Class.

A sentence or a topic outline is of value when given to the class so that the class can follow the instructor in the discussion. A topic outline is certainly better than no outline at all, as the class is much more aware of the discussion if each individual has an outline to be followed.

(c) Guide for Future Instructors.

One of the most important advantages of the topic or sentence outline is that it can be used by future instructors indicating the topics and sub-topics this instructor thought were important.

(2) *Disadvantages of Topic and Sentence Outlines.*

(a) Details not included.

Although the topic outline has the advantages indicated, the fact that the details are not included is a very definite handicap to the instructor. He has before him the main points he wants to cover but he does not have the details of his research concerning these points. It he has forgotten the points he has intended to include, he does not have them in his material for reference purposes.

(b) Research Lost for Future Use by the Instructor.

Another disadvantage of this short topic or sentence outline is that the research of the instructor has been lost for his future use. It is very doubtful that he can remember at some future time the important facts he has discovered in his research on the subject. Often the instructor is too short sighted to realize that the material will be taught again in the future. As a result, he does his research, makes the topic outline of the points he wants to cover but does not go into detail. He often feels that he should not take the time to write the outline in detail as he can remember the material for the class which will be presented in the immediate future.

(c) Other Instructors Lose Benefit of Research.

Often the instructor who has been assigned the lesson for a particular class will not be teaching this class in the future. This is especially true in police departments where the instructors are rotated. If one instructor has spent considerable time in research in a subject, future instructors should have the benefit of this research. If only a topic or sentence outline is prepared, the future instructor will have the benefit of knowing which topics were important to this instructor but will not have any details as to what he found concerning these topics. Often also, it is necessary to substitute an instructor at the last minute. If the instructor, in preparing his material, has made only a topic outline, the substitute instructor will have little to go on in presenting his material.

Manuscript Lesson Plan

Some writers state that a manuscript is not a lesson plan but a variation of the lesson plan. A manuscript lesson plan, as it will be used here, defines a complete rather than an outline plan. It contains in manuscript form everything that is to be said and is to be done in the period of instruction. The manuscript should be written for each period of instruction and kept on file for future reference.

(1) Advantages of the Manuscript Lesson Plan.

(a) Insures the Instructor that all Material will be Covered. The instructor who takes the time and effort to complete a manuscript lesson plan will be assured that all the material he feels should be covered is covered. With this complete lesson plan he can refer to specific material that he wants to be covered and include the statistics or the quotations necessary. With the manuscript lesson plan he knows that the lesson is completely prepared rather than only partially prepared.

(b) Valuable for Future Reference.

The manuscript lesson plan can be reviewed at future dates by the instructor so that all the material will be fresh in his mind. The results of his original reference study and his original analysis will have been written in detail in the manuscript lesson plan.

(c) Valuable to a New or Substitute Instructor.

The manuscript lesson plan is especially valuable to a new instructor who has been assigned a subject mater. This does not mean he will take this manuscript and use as is for his own. However, he will have benefited by the study and analysis of the instructor who completed the plan. Certainly, every police department should have on file a manuscript type lesson plan for each period of instruction. The substitute instructor will have a much less difficult task if he has a manuscript lesson plan to be used in the event of an emergency.

(2) Disadvantages of the Manuscript Lesson Plan

(a) Takes longer to prepare.

It takes the instructor much longer to prepare the manuscript type lesson plan.

(b) Danger that the instructor will read the lesson.

Often, the instructor who has prepared the complete lesson plan will feel that he has completed the lesson plan and only needs to read it to the class.

As indicated, the various types of lesson plans have their advantages and disadvantages. In the police department especially, the manuscript type of lesson plan should be used. There may be instances where the topic outline will be satisfactory if the subject is to be presented but once, and the instructor is completely familiar with the material. Generally speaking, however, the manuscript lesson plan is by far the better. The instructor could very possibly decide to use both the topic outline and the manuscript. The topic outline could be used for distribution to the class so that they can keep with the instructor on the correct topic and could be used by the instructor as a guide. A manuscript lesson plan even in this situation, should be kept for future reference and for a new or substitute instructor.

The Lesson Plan Form

There are many types of lesson plan forms used by various departments and military organizations. The important essential that a Police Training Officer must recognize is that the form used should be uniform. The department Training Officer should determine after a careful consideration, what type of lesson plan form should be used and be consistent in using this form throughout the department.

Ordinarily the lesson plan will be divided into two main parts; (a) the heading and (b) the lesson procedure.

Heading for Lesson Plan

The purpose of the *heading* for the lesson plan is to advise the instructor at a glance what the instructional unit is; time allotted to the presentation; the instructional aids, etc. Some departments have worked out forms where blocks are designated on the page for the information which defines the subject. In other words, the lesson plan form or the heading will be made up somewhat on the same order as an investigation report. Regardless of whether the heading is made up in block form or whether the information is indicated in statement form, the following information should be included in the heading. (See the sample lesson plan at the conclusion of this chapter.)

(1) Instructional Unit
   (What is the subject to be presented?)
(2) Method of Presentation.
   (What is the method or methods to be used? Lecture, conference, demonstration, practical exercise?)
(3) Time Allotted.
   (How much time has been allotted to this particular instructional unit?)
(4) Level of Class.
   (Is this to be presented to a recruit class, inservice class, supervisor's class?)

(5) References.

(What references were used by the persons who completed the lesson plan?)

(6) Training aids, Equipment and Material.

(What training aids will be required for this course and what other equipment other than the actual classroom equipment and material will be used in this course?)

(7) Assistants.

(Will assistant instructors be needed in this course and if so, how many?)

(8) Study Assignments.

(Are the students required to study outside material before the class started, if so, what are the study assignments?)

(9) Person Preparing Plan.

(What is the name of the person who prepared the lesson plan?)

(10) Date Prepared.

(On what date was the lesson plan prepared?)

The heading, of course, will not be given to the class. The heading is merely to identify the material covered in the lesson plan. The instructors in the future (or another instructor who teaches the course) will be able to identify the course, etc.

It is good practice for the Training Director to require that the heading be completed for each item indicated even though this entry would not apply in a particular course.

Lesson Procedure

This contains not only the outline of the lesson, broken down into major points and sub-points, but indicates the places where instructional aids will be used, questions asked, a review will be conducted, etc. Where the manuscript lesson plan is used, the lesson plan will also have a complete discussion of the material as it will be presented to the class.

As we indicated in a previous chapter, a complete lesson plan which employs all of the stages of instruction is divided into four parts. These four parts with their sub-divisions are listed below. Not all lesson plans will include all four parts; in fact most lesson plans will not include all four parts. If a lesson does not contain the application or examination stage of instruction, but employs only one stage of instruction, that is, the presentation stage, the main divisions of the lesson plan will then be the introduction, the body and the closing. One of the best ways to be sure the lesson is well prepared and to be sure all points are covered, is to follow the outline as presented below. This will follow the heading.

LESSON PROCEDURE   NOTES

I. PRESENTATION. (The method of presentation and the approximate time for the presentation).

    A. Introduction. (Time required for introduction).

    Note: If at this point the instructor intends to use some attention-getting demonstration or skit, this should be placed here in the form of a "note" in the lesson plan.

       1. Objective. (State here the objective or purpose of this period of instruction).

       2. Reasons. (Give the reasons why the students should learn this particular lesson by stressing its importance and application).

       3. Review. (The instructor will review previous instruction, if any, which is related or tied in with this period of instruction).

       4. Procedure. (Indicate procedure that will be followed by the instructor in presenting the material to the class).

    B. Body. (Time required)

    In the body or explanation, the teaching points will be presented in a designated order. The first teaching point should be designated as "1," Sub-points, "a,b,c." The same sequence of numbering should be followed in presenting each teaching point and sub-points.

    When notes, training aids, questions and other instructional procedures are to be used, they should be put in the plan as a reminder to the instructor in the order as follows.

LESSON PROCEDURE

Question: What are the principles of learning?

Note: Use training aids No. 6.

Example: Tell the story of a poorly trained police officer.

If a demonstration is used, the demonstration should be completely described in the lesson plan including the type of equipment to be used, and when and how this equipment will be used.

C. Closing. (Time required)

The closing should consist of three parts which will be described on the following page. The closing has a definite purpose as indicated in previous chapters and should not be omitted. The parts of the closing, which should be used as necessary, are as follows:

1. Summary.

In the summary, the instructor briefly summarizes the main points and subpoints that have been presented in this lesson.

2. Questions from the Class.

Here the instructor gives the students an opportunity to clear up any questions they might have concerning the presentation.

3. Closing Statement.

The closing statement should leave the student with the feeling that he has learned something in this class.

II. Application.

If the lesson or period of instruction is to include practical work on the part of the student, this should be clearly defined in this section of the lesson plan. As in the presentation, this should be carefully outlined and each step to be taken by the instructor included in the lesson plan. Some principles which should be applied by the instructor in this phase of the lesson plan are as follows:

A. Give complete direction to the students.

LESSON PROCEDURE   NOTES

B. Have a general plan for conduct of the practical work.
C. Determine how the students will be arranged for the practical work.
D. Determine whether assistants needed to complete the practical work.
E. Specify the exact procedure to be followed.
F. Emphasize the safety precautions to be observed.

Of course, other points should be covered so the instructor will be reminded exactly what he must do in this application stage of instruction.

III. Examination.

If any type of the evaluation is to be used, it should be clearly stated in the lesson plan. If the written test is to be used, it could be included as an annex to the plan. If an oral test is to be used, the question to be included should either be in the lesson plan or as an annex. If the observation type of evaluation is to be used, a check sheet should have been prepared in advance and be included as an annex to the plan.

IV. Critique.

The critique, as we discussed, has a specific purpose. As indicated in previous chapters, it is difficult to plan for the critique. However, the lesson plan can include the steps the instructor should follow in conducting the critique. These are:

A. Restate the objective of the lesson.
B. Evaluate performance.
C. Guide the class in group discussion of the lesson.
D. Make a summary of the points covered.

If only one of two of the stages of instruction as outlined above, are to be used in any one subject, a breakdown within that one stage should still be followed. For example, if the instructor is teaching only one hour on Techniques of Arrest and interested only in the presentation stage of instruction, he will still include the introduction, the body, and the closing. A complete teaching unit should include all the stages of instruction as outlined above.

Making the Lesson Plan

Some guides will help the instructor in making a more usable plan. Some suggestions are enumerated below for consideration by the instructor.

Use Correct Designation of Topics

The instructor should be certain that the topics are designated as correctly as possible. He should try to select words or phrases which will designate the material that will be covered under each topic or sub-topic. This not only assists the students but keeps the instructor on the right track.

The topics and sub-topics should be correctly designated numerically. There are several approved methods for designating topics and breaking down the subject matter. Any method can be used, but this should be consistent. One approved method of breaking down subject matter is as follows:

I.
  A.
    1
      a
        (1)
          (a)
  B.
II.
  A.
  B.

In breaking down material, there should be at least two headings in each order. For example, if there is a capital "A" under Roman Numeral I, there should also be a "B." The topic is not divided unless there are at least two parts to this topic.

Select Main Topics and Sub-Topics

The instructor must use care in determining which of the topics he will give the most weight. It takes some experience to correctly divide the material into correct topics and sub-topics. The topics designated should be of relatively equal importance and the sub-topics must logically come under the main topics. The sub-topics should be supporting or explanatory and should be related to the main point and helpful in developing its meaning. The main points of the lesson or the teaching points of the lesson are expressed in the main topics. These are the points the student must learn if he is to fulfill the requirements established by the instructor. These points should be mutually related, coordinated and arranged progressively.

Show Teaching Procedures

The purpose of the lesson plan is not only to present the teaching points logically and progressively but to help the instructor in following the procedure he has planned to follow. A lesson plan should show when such things as training aids, summaries, and questions are to be used in the lesson plan. The use of the training aids will have meaning if used in exactly the right place while they might lose their meaning if used too late or too early. The lesson plan should show clearly where training aids or other aids for the instructor will be used.

Make a USABLE Lesson Plan

The lesson plan is the tool the instructor will use in presenting the material to the class. It should be the best tool possible. It is a good idea to make the lesson plan double spaced so that it is easy to follow. In fact, if a large type typewriter is available, this should be used as the instructor then can get further away from his lesson and still use the plan. Paragraphs should be indented so they will be easily ascertained. Underscoring is often helpful in reminding the instructor of the specific points he wants to emphasize. It is also a good idea to leave marginal space so that the instructor can write notes which will help him in emphasizing certain points. In other words, the instructor should make the lesson plan a workable plan.

Using the Lesson Plan

The lesson plan is the outline for teaching. It keeps the pertinent material before the instructor and insures order and unity in presentation. The lesson plan keeps the instructor from getting off the beam. It keeps the instructor from omitting essential points and introducing irrelevant points.

The students appreciate an instructor who has given attention to the teaching points and has carefully prepared the lesson.

This does *not* mean that the instructor will read ver-batem without emphasis. It does *not* mean that the instructor is finished when he has completed the lesson plan. He still must think while teaching. Some suggestions for the instructor as to the use of the lesson plan are as follows:

Follow the Lesson Plan

The instructor should have the lesson plan available at all times for quick reference. It should, however, be held in his hand only when actually necessary. When the lesson plan gets in the way of the instructor and the students are more aware of it than learning, the lesson plan has lost its value.

Review the Lesson Before Class Time

As we pointed out, one of the values of a complete lesson plan is that the instructor can completely review it and have the teaching points in mind before the class starts. A review of the material puts the teaching points at the command of the instructor, and eliminates unnecessary pauses in teaching.

Adapt the Plan to Learning Situation

The instructor often finds in presenting the lesson that the suggested procedures are not leading to the desired results. If this happens, he should feel free to change the approach; keeping in mind, however, that there are certain teaching points which must be presented. Each class is different, and no matter how careful the planning, it is impossible to predict with complete certainty the reaction of different classes. Therefore the plan should be flexible enough so that a variation in procedures can be made if necessary. If the instructor is using a lesson plan prepared by another instructor, he must make this lesson plan *his* lesson plan. He will, no doubt, use different wording and different examples than the other instructor.

Keep the Plan up to Date

The instructor who repeatedly uses the unchanged plan year after year will lower his efficiency. This is especially true if dates or statistics are used and the instructor has not taken the necessary action to change these. Also the students will change and the instructor must make the plan to fit the level of the students. The instructor must also keep his plan up to date by making use of more effective procedures, new training aids, and new teaching techniques.

LESSON PLAN

In making the lesson plan, the instructor should refer to discussion of the lesson plan form. This form or adaptations of this form will, if followed consistently, insure the instructor of a logical presentation.

Included here is a sample lesson plan made for a short period of presentation. This includes the heading and lesson outline. Also included are the first pages of lesson plan forms used by other departments indicating how the heading can be made in block form. When a lesson plan form has been selected by a department, directions should be given the instructors on how to make a lesson plan and the lesson plan form should be followed consistently.

Sample Lesson Plan

(Sample)

INSTRUCTIONAL UNIT	*The Crime Scene Investigation*
METHOD OF PRESENTATION	Conference
TIME ALLOTED	20 Minutes
LEVEL OF CLASS	Recruit Class
REFERENCES	Kirk, Paul L., *Crime Investigation*, Fitzgerald, M. A., *Criminal Investigation*
TRAINING AIDS, EQUIPMENT AND MATERIAL	Venetian blind, slides for venetian blind, overhead projector, and transparancies.
ASSISTANTS	Assistant instructor to operate overhead projector
STUDY ASSIGNMENTS	None.
PERSON PREPARING PLAN	Lieutenant John H. Williams
DATE PREPARED	March 12, 1962

LESSON PROCEDURE	NOTES
A. INTRODUCTION (2 Minutes) *Note*: Tell story of case that was lost because the officer failed to protect the evidence found at a crime scene. 1. Objective. During this period we shall dis-	

LESSON PROCEDURE	NOTES

cuss the proper procedures to be followed in making an investigation at the scene of a crime.

2. Reasons. Every police officer, whether he is a beat officer, detective, supervisor or special investigator, has the responsibility of learning the basic procedures in making a crime scene investigation. Even though he is not given the assignment of investigating crimes, he may encounter a situation where he is the only officer at the scene. If the proper steps are not taken at the right time, future action may be too late.

3. Review. In previous classes we have discussed the methods of investigation and how to make notes. In this lesson we shall continue with the procedures to be followed at the crime scene and will, in the future lessons, discuss the use of evidence found at the crime scene.

4. Procedure. In this lesson, we shall use a hypothetical situation and discuss the steps which should be followed by the officer at the crime scene. The steps to be discussed are:
   1. Start record upon arrival at scene.
   2. Clear the crime scene and secure witnesses.
   3. Isolate the crime scene.
   4. Secure all available information.
   5. Search for and preserve all evidence.

B. BODY. (16 minutes)

Note: Use venetian blind.
      Give details of hypothetical situation.

1. Start record upon arrival at scene.
   a. Record the exact time and date of arrival.

LESSON PROCEDURE	NOTES

    b. Record exact weather conditions.

    c. Record exact address and location of the crime.

    d. Record all other information which may be important in making further investigation or in presenting the case in court.

2. Clear crime scene and secure witnesses.

    a. Arrest subject if he is present.

    b. Tactfully remove family, witnesses, and public from scene.

    c. Obtain names and addresses of all witnesses so they can be contacted later.

    d. Talk to eye-witnesses at the time for information to aid in the investigation. Depending upon the situation it may be advisable to wait until a later time to get detailed statements.

3. Isolate the crime scene.

    Note: Use transparency # 1. (Indicates the proper way to isolate the crime scene.)

    a. If inside, post a guard at each entrance or lock the doors in order that only authorized persons are allowed to enter.

    b. If outside, rope all areas, post guards, get spectators back, etc.

4. Secure all available information.

    Note: Question to Class. When should photographs be taken?

    a. Make photographs before anything is moved and record in the notebook complete identifying information concerning each photograph.

        (1) Close-up photograph of body from all angles.

        (2) Photographs showing the entire room; one from each corner and each side of the room.

LESSON PROCEDURE	NOTES

(3) Photographs of possible avenues of escape if applicable.

b. Make notes giving full description of body (if homicide case) including description of clothing, condition of clothing, name of person, and all other identifying information including weight, height, color of hair and eyes, type and location of wounds, etc. Remember, no officer has ever been punished for getting too much.

c. Make complete notes describing everything in the room.

(1) Show position of body.

(2) Describe position of weapon in relation to body.

(3) Indicate arrangement of furniture.

(4) Include condition of furniture, room, etc.

(5) Record information concerning any other possible evidence such as broken glass, blood, bottles, etc.

It should be pointed out that each crime scene will be different. All of the points mentioned would obviously not be present in every crime scene but this should act as a guide and remind the investigator that he must make the record complete.

d. Make a diagram of the crime scene.

Note: Use transparency # 2. (Diagram of a crime scene).

(1) Include all openings in room and direction of opening.

(2) Have all furniture in diagram.

(3) Include all measurements such as size of room, exact location of body, exact location of any weapon, etc.

(4) Make diagram to scale at later time.

LESSON PROCEDURE	NOTES

(5) Be sure that the diagram agrees with facts recorded in notebook.

    e. Make a diagram of the immediate area around the crime scene.

      Note: Use transparency # 3. (Diagram of area outside house).

(1) Show area immediately adjacent to room, house, yard or building.

(2) Indicate location of streets, avenue of escape, etc.

(3) Include on diagram location of evidence found outside of immediate crime area.

5. Search for and preserve *all* evidence.

After photographs have been taken and the diagram has been completed, the investigator should consider the following steps in making a more thorough search.

    a. Move the body and make a complete search of body, clothing, etc.

    b. Process scene for latent prints.

    c. Mark all evidence and place in proper containers.

    d. Search possible avenues of escape.

C. Closing. (2 Minutes)

1. Summary. Every police officer should be familiar with the procedures to be followed in making a crime scene investigation. In this period we have discussed five steps which the investigator should remember in order to complete the investigation satisfactorily and to prepare his case for court. As was pointed out, these steps are not intended to be exclusive but to serve as a guide. The steps discussed were:

    Note: Use venetian blind for review of main points.

LESSON PROCEDURE	NOTES
a. Start record upon arrival at scene. b. Clear the crime scene and secure witness-es. c. Isolate the crime scene. d. Secure all available information. e. Search for and preserve all evidence. 2. Questions from the class. *Note:* Ask the members of the class if there are any questions concerning the material covered. 3. Closing Statement. If the investigation at the crime scene is conducted properly, there is a good chance that the investigation will be completed satisfactorily and the guilty party convicted in court. But if this first step is not handled correctly, no amount of future investigation can correct the errors. THE COURT CASE IS NO BETTER THAN THE INVESTIGATOR.	

CLOSING

Summary

In this chapter entitled, "Making the Lesson Plan," we have discussed purposes of the lesson plan, types of lesson plans, lesson plan forms, procedures to be followed in making the lesson plan, recommendations concerning the use of the lesson plan. We learned that the lesson plan has many advantages and purposes including the certainty of coverage, the correct sequence, time control and that the lesson plan gives confidence to the instructor.

We learned that there are several types of lesson plans, each of these types having advantages and disadvantages and that the instructors must select the one most suitable for his purpose. In the discussion of the lesson plan form, we emphasized the parts of the lesson plan and the elements which should be included in each lesson plan. We further discussed some procedures to be followed in making a lesson plan and lastly some of the suggestions for the instructor to follow in making use of the lesson plan.

We closed our discussion with samples of the lesson plan which can serve as a guide for instructors.

KENTUCKY STATE POLICE
TRAINING

LESSON PLAN

Lesson Title		Page 1 of _____ pages
Course		Hours

Synopsis:

Objectives:

Student References or Assignments:	Instructor References:
Training Aids:	Issue Material:

KSP — TR Form No. 26

METROPOLITAN POLICE DEPARTMENT — CITY OF ST. LOUIS
TRAINING DIVISION

LESSON PLAN

Course	Date Prepared	Subject	....Pages
	Prepared By		....Hours
Hours	Lesson Title	Last Date Revised	
		Revised By	

Scope

Objective

| Student References | Instructor |
| Instructional Aids | Issue Material |

Closing Statement

Properly used lesson plans insure complete coverage. The instructor who plans well and uses his plan wisely, seldom runs out of time or omits important items. When an instructor has developed a complete lesson plan, he has taught the lesson to himself before teaching it to his students. The lesson plan to an instructor is just as important as the scalpel to a surgeon, the slide rule to an engineer, or the law books to an attorney.

Chapter 10

SUPERVISION OF INSTRUCTION

INTRODUCTION

Reasons for Chapter

Every function within the police department must be supervised. In order for the police operations to be effective, the program must be so organized that each man in the unit knows to whom he should look for supervision. This is also true of the training program. Someone in the department must be responsible for effective training. In addition to applying the general techniques and principles of supervision, there are certain specific guides which will help the police training supervisor in evaluating instructor performance.

Objectives

We shall analyze the aspects of supervision so as to develop a better understanding of the purposes, principles and steps in supervising instructors.

Review

In previous chapters we have discussed how a lesson plan should be completed and presented and have learned some of the characteristics of a good instructor. In this chapter we shall discuss some principles to be followed in determining if the lesson plan has been presented in accordance with the policies of the department.

Procedure

In order to make the contents of this chapter more easily understood, the material has been divided into six parts: (1) The Responsibility for Supervision of Instruction in the Police Department. (2) Purposes of Supervision. (3) Planning for Supervision. (4) Principles in Supervising the Instructors. (5) Evaluating the Instructor, and (6) The use of the Rating Scale in determining effectiveness.

BODY

The Responsibility for Supervision of Instruction in the Police Department

Unfortunately, in many police departments the responsibility for training has not been fixed and as a result, training is hap-hazard. In order for training to be effective, a well qualified person must be placed in charge of the training program and be responsible for it. Of course, the Chief or the principal administrator in the department, is generally responsible for training. However, this responsibility is usually delegated to a training officer. The training officer not only has the responsibility of determining what subjects shall be taught in the training school and determining who shall do the instructing but he is also responsible for training the instructors and supervising the instruction. This responsibility should be fixed, even in a small department.

Purposes of Supervision

Many instructors consider supervision to be the policing aspect of administration. If supervision is to be effective, this conception must be destroyed. The supervisor must exert every possible effort to develop the conception that supervision is a helping process. Some of the specific purposes of supervision in the police training school are as follows:

To Determine the Effectiveness of Instruction

Obviously the primary purpose of supervision is to determine if the student has learned the material being taught. As we indicated earlier if the student has not learned, the instructor has not taught. It follows that the instructor has not used the proper teaching techniques. On the other hand, if the student is learning the material, supervisors should not be too quick to critize if the method is logical.

To Assist the Instructor in Improving his Instructional Abilities

The person who supervises the instruction should be alert in selecting the areas where the instructor can improve. Of course, the supervisor must himself be a well-qualified instructor. The supervisor must guard against prescribing a set formula for every teacher. It is a mistake for the supervisor to "wrap up" a set of instructions, neatly label them and insist that each instructor follow these to the letter. This could easily bring about a type of uniformity that is not conducive to good teaching.

To Assist the Instructor in Analyzing Instructional Problems

The purpose of supervision is not that of "telling what to do in certain situations" but rather one of helping the teacher learn what the problems are and then determining the best methods of solving them.

To Keep the Instructors Advised Concerning New Aids and Techniques

As in other fields, teaching techniques are being developed every day. Techniques used by the instructor today may not be satisfactory several years from now. Therefore, the supervisor has the responsibility of seeing that the instructors are kept up to date concerning new techniques and procedures. In order to do this, the supervisor himself must be always alert to new methods and procedures in training.

To Determine if Additional Instruction is Necessary

The supervisor cannot assume that every instructor will be qualified. The instructor should have been trained as an instructor before he is given the responsibility of training. If the supervisor finds that the instructor is not using the proper methods and is not accomplishing the objectives, it may be necessary to give that instructor additional training in the techniques of instruction.

To Determine if the General Training Objectives Are Being Accomplished

The overall purpose of supervision of instructors is to determine if the training objectives of the department are being accomplished. If these training objectives are not being accomplished, it will be necessary for the supervisor to determine the reasons why they are not and to take effective steps to remedy this situation.

The above are some of the purposes of supervision and some of the reasons why the instructors should be supervised. These, of course, are not all inclusive, however, these do indicate that it is necessary that instructors be supervised and that someone be assigned this responsibility.

Planning for Supervision

Good supervision is planned supervision. Every enterprize to be successful, must be preceded by a plan. This is just as true in the field of supervision of instruction. In planning the supervisory visit, the supervisor should apply the following general principles.

Determine the Purpose of the Visit

The supervisor who goes into the classroom "cold," without any purpose is disturbing the class and accomplishing very little. He should not go in with the idea of looking around to see what he can find wrong but should have a purpose in mind.

Prepare a Schedule of Visits

A supervisor who haphazardly visits classes without any planned schedule will not get an overall picture of the training program. This does not mean he has to advise the instructor in advance that he will be there or that he cannot deviate from the schedule. However, to be sure that all instructors are visited, he should have his schedule planned well in advance.

Determine the Items to be Inspected and Observed

In order to be effective and uniform in the supervision of instruction, the supervisor should determine in advance exactly what items he shall inspect. For example, he might decide that he would like to inspect the appearance of the instructor, the instructor's ability to get along with his students, the instructor's speech techniques, etc. Or he might determine that he wants to observe if the instructor is properly using training aids or if the instruction is generally effective.

Prepare a Check List

Just as the investigator who investigates a crime has a check list to be sure that he accomplished every thing he intends to do, so, too, should the supervisor have a check list to be sure he has observed and evaluated the items he has intended to observe and evaluate. Without a check list, he is apt to forget or over-look some of the points with the result that the evaluation will not be comprehensive.

Principles in Supervision

In addition to the general supervisory principles which should also be followed in supervising of instruction, there are some specific supervisory principles which should be employed. Here we will only mention the most outstanding of these principles. Some of them are as follows:

Recognize Individual Differences

The supervisor must recognize that an instructor can be effective in his instruction and yet not use the same techniques as other instructors. If the basic instructional techniques are followed, the supervisor should not criticize merely because the instructor is not using the same techniques that he, the supervisor, would use.

Be Courteous

The best procedure is for the supervisor to identify himself to the instructor in charge prior to the start of the period of instruction, making as little "fuss" about entering the room as possible and take a seat in the rear of the room. The supervisor should regard himself as a guest of the instructor and should accord him the appropriate courtesy.

Have a Desire to Improve Instruction

The supervisor should not merely attempt to find fault but should approach the visit with a positive point of view.

Correct Errors in Private

One of the best ways to destroy the rapport between the instructor and supervisor is to correct an error while the instruction is taking place in the classroom. If a supervisor detects an error in the actual facts being presented, he should not correct the error at that time but advise the instructor at a later time and let him correct the error in the next class. The only possible exception to this would be in a situation where an error would involve a life and death matter and there is no possibility of the instructor correcting the error at a later date. Unless the supervisor is invited to participate in the discussion, he should not volunteer answers or take any part in the discussion in class.

Treat the Instructor As You Would Want to be Treated

The supervisor who follows this general rule will be a more

successful supervisor. On the other hand, the supervisor who is arrogant, who attempts to find fault, who is discourteous, who causes an instructor to "lose face" before the students, will do more harm than good.

Evaluating the Instructor

The instructors are required to evaluate the students. The purpose is to determine if the students are learning the material being presented. Also, the supervisor of instruction must evaluate the effectiveness of the teacher. Observation of the teacher's approach by the supervisor is of little value if the instructor is not given the benefit of the supervisor's evaluation. The immediate goal of all evaluation of instructors is to plan experiences that will promote instructor growth.

The supervisor in his observation has checked each specific item that he has planned to observe. He should have determined which part of the activity was conducted in an "outstanding," "satisfactory," or "poor" manner. In making this evaluation the supervisor must compare what was accomplished by the teacher with what reasonbly could have been expected under the circumstances existing at the time.

Probably the best practice is to have a conference with the instructor at some pre-arranged time after the observation of the instruction. Even though the instruction was satisfactory, the conference should be held if only to tell the instructor that he did perform satisfactorily. If the supervisor determines that the instructor should have accomplished more, a conference should be set up to discuss with the instructor the specific ways in which his instruction could be improved. In conducting the conference with the instructor, the supervisor should keep the principle of good supervision in mind. Some of the specific principles to be followed, if the rapport between the instructor and supervisor is to be kept on a high level, are as follows:

Study All the Information Available Concerning the Instructor in Order to Get Better Acquainted with his Background

The supervisor will be much more able to discuss matters with the instructor if he understands the past experiences of the instructor.

Determine in Advance What is Desired to be Accomplished in the Conference

To be beneficial, the conference must be purposeful. It must not be haphazard but have a definite purpose.

Place Emphasis on the Growth of the Individual

Let the instructor know that the purpose of the conference is to improve instruction and not to criticize him as an individual. Avoid indications that the conference is for disciplinary purposes.

Treat the Opinion of the Instructor with Respect

Let the instructor understand that the supervisor's opinion or evaluation is not unalterable. Avoid giving the impression that the supervisors are always right and the instructors are always wrong.

Emphasize Strong Characteristics

Be sincere in extending compliments concerning the good work that the instructor has done. It is often tempting to "jump right in" and start discussing the weak points. If the supervisor intends to have a good working relationship with the instructor, he must be sincere in pointing out the good as well as points which need improving.

Center the Conference on the Instructor-learning Situation

Avoid discussing the instructor as a person. Rather, keep the discussion concerning performance and the necessity of improving the instruction.

Keep the Discussion Confidential

All matters discussed in individual conferences must be kept in strict professional confidence. Not only must the conference be conducted in private but the matters discussed should be kept strictly confidential.

Be Specific in Recommendations

A supervisor in planning a conference must have prepared in advance the specific areas in which he feels the instructor should improve. These are based upon a check sheet that was used when he observed the instructor. If, after the interview, the supervisor still feels that these points need improving, he should be specific in discussing these with the instructor. A suggestion to improve, generally, will be of very little benefit, but if, the instructor knows specifically in which areas he can improve, he can concentrate on these areas.

Draw From the Instructor Possible Solutions of Problems

Rather than suggesting methods of improving, more positive results will be obtained if the supervisor can get the instructor to think through methods of improvement.

End Each Conference With an Understanding as to What is to be Done

End the conference with a positive note as to what the instructor can do to improve. It might be a good idea to review the points discussed so that these can be fixed in the instructor's mind.

Make a Conscious Effort to Learn From the Instructor

The interview should be a two-way process. Not only will the instructor benefit but the supervisor will also grow.

In order to determine if the instructor is making progress, it is necessary that a supervisor keep cumulative records of individual supervisory conferences. With this record, the supervisor can determine in a later follow-up period of observation if the instructor is carrying out the suggestions made by the supervisor. Also, over a period of time the instructor should be able to determine if the instructor has benefited by the conferences.

The Use of Rating Scales in Determining Effectiveness

We have indicated in earlier parts of this chapter that it is necessary for the supervisor to know exactly what he is looking for when he observes instructors carrying instructional responsibilities. We also stated that in order to conduct an interview properly, the supervisor must have specific points to be discussed and specific recommendations to make. To assist in accomplishing these things, rating scales or evaluation sheets have been prepared by various schools and colleges. These serve a very definite purpose. However, it should not be implied that it is possible to construct a definite yardstick with which to measure the effectiveness of all teachers or instructors. There are two reasons why one single rating scale will not serve to measure the effectiveness of all instructors. One, the human factors in the teaching situation are all variables, thus forming an impossible base upon which

INSTRUCTOR RATING SCALE

Instructor_____ Subject Area_____

Rater_____ Date_____ Rating_____

DIRECTIONS: Each item of the scale is scored on a basis of 10 points. These points are grouped under headings of "Superior," "Excellent," "Good," "Fair" and "Poor." The higher scores indicate the higher proficiency in performance.

SUPERIOR   Highest possible score.

EXCELLENT   Characteristic or ability is above average.

GOOD   Characteristic or ability is acceptable in every respect.

FAIR   Characteristic or ability is below average and not entirely acceptable.

POOR   Definite improvement must be shown to be acceptable.

	9.00-10	7-8.99	4-6.99	2-3.99	1-1.99
	Superior	Excellent	Good	Fair	Poor

A. The Instructor:
1. Personal Characteristics
  Appearance and Bearing
  Physical Vitality
  Voice
  Poise and Confidence
  Emotional Balance
2. Professional Characteristics
  Command of English
  Mastery of Subject Matter
  Mastery of Training
    Technicians					

B. The Instructor-Student Relations: 1. Cooperative Attitude 2. Individual Differences Considered 3. Motivation of Students 4. Students Treated Impartially 5. Student Interest					

C. Class Procedure:
1. Reasons and Objections
  Stated
2. Interest Developed
3. Lesson Organized
4. Material Vitalized
5. Training Aids
  Used Effectively
6. Students' Questions
  Answered
7. Points of Lesson Emphasized
8. Demonstration Used
  Where Practical					

D. Classroom 1. Neat and Clean 2. Unnecessary Equipment Removed 3. Proper Ventilation					

to establish a constant measure. Two, rating scales are composed of many items. It would be impossible for an instructor to conduct himself in such a manner that they would all be applicable to him on any one day.

In spite of the fact that no fool-proof scale has been prepared, rating scales can be used effectively if the supervisor realizes that these are just one tool in the evaluation process. The reader who has attempted to devise a rating scale for rating employee effectiveness will understand the problem of trying to devise an instructor rating scale.

To assist the police instructor in conducting his own grading scale which meets the needs of his particular department, the rating scale on the preceding page is given to serve as a guide.

It can be seen that this rating scale can be used primarily by the supervisor as a check list and as a guide in helping him in rating the instructor and in discussing performance with the instructor. In order to have an over-all rating for the instructor on this type of rating sheet, it is necessary for the instructor to somewhat subjectively reach this rating. It would be unfair to add all of these ratings and come up with an average, as some of the characteristics or items rated are much more important than others.

Many types of rating scales or check sheets are available. The instructor should choose the one that will accomplish his purpose most adequately. It is emphasized however that some type or rating list should be used in order that the supervisor will have a system which is uniform and fair to all concerned.

CLOSING

Summary

In this chapter we have discussed the supervisor and his responsibilities in supervising the instructors. It is necessary that all instructors be supervised in order to insure that departmental policies are carried out that learning is actually taking place. In this chapter we have discussed the responsibility for supervision in the training program, the purposes of supervision, some points to remember in planning supervision, principles to be followed by the instructor should be evaluated and a rating scale that can be used by the supervisor in supervising the instructors.

Closing Statement

If policing is to become professionalized, qualified men must be appointed and properly trained. Without proper training, many unnecessary mistakes will be made by police officers. If training is to be conducted effectively and efficiently, the responsibility for training must be placed in a well qualified person and training must be properly supervised. Supervision is just as essential in the police training school as in the field.

Chapter 11

OBJECTIVES AND CONTENT OF DEPARTMENTAL TRAINING PROGRAM

INTRODUCTION

Reasons for Chapter

In order for the police instructor to adequately establish a training program for the department, he must evaluate the objectives of this program; he must determine what subjects are necessary to carry out the objectives of the training program and the department.

Objective of Chapter

The purpose of this chapter is to discuss the objectives of the departmental training program and to point out some of the subjects that should be included in the training program.

Review of Previous Instruction

We have discussed in previous chapters the processes of learning, the foundations on which learning takes place, and the steps the instructor should take in preparing and presenting the subject matter. It is also important to select the best subject matter for the needs of the dapartment.

Procedure

This chapter is divided into two parts. The first part deals with the objectives of the training program and the various phases of the training program; the second part discusses the content of the various phases of the training program.

BODY

Objectives of the Departmental Training Program

General Objectives of Departmental Training Program

(1) *Recruit Training.*

Unlike some of the other professions, the ordinary police recruit has received very little if any preemployment training. The procedure of selection in most departments has developed however to the extent that the men selected have the capacity to learn to be good law enforcement agents. One of the primary objectives of the police instructor then is to make an efficient law enforcement officer from a qualified but untrained recruit.

(2) *Inservice Retraining.*

Training of the recruit is only one of the general objectives of the training program. Laws change and procedures change. To maintain an efficient organization, training must be a continuing process. Too often in some of our police organizations, the recruit is better trained than the officer who has been working many years without retraining. Another very important function of the Departmental training program is to conduct regular retraining programs which will make all of the officers acquainted with new procedures and new laws. In order to do this, it is necessary to maintain records on each person indicating his training status.

(3) *Supervisory Training.*

Probably the area that is most neglected in the police training program is the preparation of supervisors. The supervisor's responsibilities are so different than the non-supervisors that it is essential that the supervisor receive additional training before assuming supervisory duties.

(4) *Training of Specialists.*

In discussing the objectives of the training program we must consider also the training of specialists in the department. The modern police departments must have personnel who are especially trained for specific duties. In some instances this type of training can be secured more economically outside of the department but in others this must also be conducted by the training staff within the department.

(5) *Training of Administrators.*

Administrators must also be trained. The practice in by far of the majority of police agencies is to promote higher administrative officers from within the department. While it is true that much knowledge concerning administration is learned on the job, it is essential that training in administration be made available to the new administrator. Often this type of training can also be secured more adequately outside of the department but the officer in charge of the training program should consider the possibility of offering this in the departmental training program.

(6) *Instructor Training.*

In the modern police department, training takes place not only in the police academy but is an every day process at every level of supervision. To adequately convey ideas to others, every supervisor should be trained in the methods of instruction. To accomplish this, the training program for the department should include a course in methods or techniques of instruction. One of the purposes of the previous chapters of this book is to furnish material and procedure for conducting this type of training.

These six general areas for training in the police agency should not be considered as excluding others. The training officers must always be alert to determine if training is desirable in other areas. He must remember that the police function is always changing. To a great extent the efficiency of the department depends upon the ability of the training officer in determining where training is needed and in giving this training in an effective and efficient manner.

Specific Objectives of the Police Program

(1) Make proper administration of the department possible. The student must be taught first in recruit school and in the other parts of the training program the necessity of discipline and the rules and regulations of the department which he must follow. In no other occupation is there more necessity for strict compliance to rules and regulations. This must be emphasized in the training program.

Also the organization of the department must be known by the officer in order that he might see how he fits into the organization and the big purpose of the organization.

(2) Develop a thorough understanding of our system of Government. The police officer must know the history of our system of Government, a Government that strives to protect society as well as to protect the rights of the individual. He must

understand the authority and limitations of the Federal Government and how the municipal and state governments get their power. Without this he will not understand what his proper place is as a law enforcement officer.

(3) Develop a knowledge of the laws and ordinances and the elements of each offense. In addition to knowing the laws which give the police officer authority to act, he must know the elements that must be proved in order to obtain a conviction. Too often cases are lost because the officer did not have a complete knowledge of each element of the offense or has made an incorrect charge.

(4) Teach the officer to avoid illegal acts. The police officer is placed in a position where he is required to act but must act within his legal authority. There is often a fine line between what is legal and illegal. In our complex society, it is necessary that the police officer protect society and yet protect individual rights. To do this the police officer must be very thoroughly trained in law. It is not exaggerating to say that he must know criminal law as well or better than the average attorney.

(5) Prepare men to perform duties with confidence and safety. The untrained police officer can not perform his duties with confidence. Much of the criticism of police has been brought about because the police officer has not applied safety methods in enforcing the law. Confidence goes hand and hand with knowledge, preparation and experience. In the training phase the instructor can do much to build up the confidence of the police officer by using practical exercises and teaching the officer exactly what he can and cannot do.

(6) Develop patrol techniques. The training school has the initial responsibility of developing techniques that will be used on foot patrol or automobile patrol. This will of course include many subject areas such as purposes, types, observation and recognition, proper methods of apprehension, operation of automobiles, etc.

(7) Develop investigation techniques. The police officer has many and varied duties. Among these duties is the duty to properly investigate offences, obtain the evidence, interview wit-

nesses, make accurate reports and complete other duties necessary to the proper preparation of cases for court.

(8) Develop courtroom techniques. If the guilty violator is not fined or imprisoned due to the failure of the police officer to properly present the facts in court, the apprehension is meaningless; in fact, harmful. The training section has the initial responsibility to so train the officer that he can present the material in court with ease and confidence.

(9) Develop an understanding of human behavior. To properly work with an individual or to control mob action when the need arises, the officer should have a basic knowledge of human behavior. He should have knowledge of mental illness, character disorders and human relations. Some recruits will have had training in these areas but many will not.

(10) Promote an understanding of the necessity of good public relations. The training personnel can do much to improve the status of the department by teaching that the relations between the public and the department determine the effectiveness of the department as well as the salaries and working conditions of the department personnel. The officer must be made to understand that every member of the department is a representative of the department and has a public relations function.

(11) Provide the recruit a basis for further learning. A qualified person plus recruit training will not make a finished police officer. The recruit training will, however, provide the basis on which the officer can learn. The recruit training is only the beginning. The officer should be made aware that in the police function, learning is continuous.

(12) Give the recruit a lasting impression concerning law enforcement. No two recruits on entering the department have the same conceptions of law enforcement. The impressions, the appreciations, the ideals that are developed in the recruit training program will be, to a very large extent, lasting. If the proper appreciations are developed in the recruit school, the standards of the department can only go higher.

In preparing the course of instruction, the training officer must keep these objectives in view. To overlook any one of these objectives will result in the omission of some subject that should be included in the curriculum.

Again it must be pointed out that particular departments will have other objectives. No two departments will have the same needs. The alert training officer must evaluate the specific objectives before selecting the subject matter.

Content of Departmental Program

Subjects offered in the training school will vary from state to state and department to department. To a great extent the purpose of the department, the type of community, the peculiar problems of the area, the background of the employees of the department, and other factors will determine the content of the departmental training program. No fast rule can be stated as to what subjects should be taught or how much emphasis should be placed on each subject. This is as it should be in our form of government where the police function is decentralized.

Many police administrators have argued that the same subjects should be taught in every police training school. This would to some extent standardize procedures and in this respect is very desirable. But as long as the problems of the individual communities and states are different, some subjects will be included in some training programs and not in others.

The purpose of the second part of this chapter is to submit a group of subjects that should usually be included in the training program. Most of these are basic and should be included in all police training programs. In some cases, however, the chief administrator and training officer must determine which of the subjects should not be included and include other subjects to properly prepare the officer to carry out his duties. These subjects should in all cases be given careful consideration by those responsible for training.

Recruit Training

At the present time most of the men entering police service have had no police training. These men with the mental capacity to learn must be given basic police training before they can perform any police service. In those departments where college work in policing is required, the recruit training program must necessarily be adjusted but some initial training will always be necessary.

The following subjects are suggested for inclusion in the recruit training program. Obviously, these are only suggested subjects as the subjects included will vary to meet the needs of individual departments.

The subjects are listed under eight classifications as a matter of organization. Other methods of breaking down the subjects into areas could be easily justified. Also it should be noted that some subjects pertain to areas other than the ones under which they are listed. For example; "Reporting writing" is included under Patrol Techniques while it could have been included in one of the other headings.

(1) Administrative Procedures
    (a) Study Techniques and Notetaking
    (b) Organization of the Police Agency
    (c) Functions of the Bureaus within the Agency
    (d) Rules and Regulations of the Agency
    (e) Civil Service Provisions
    (f) Personnel and Disciplinary Procedures
    (g) Functions of Other Law Enforcement Agencies
    (h) Physical Training
    (i) Law Enforcement Code and Cannons of Ethics

(2) Laws and Criminal Procedures
    (a) Fundamentals of Criminal Law
    (b) Constitutional Law
    (c) History of Policing
    (d) Laws of Arrest, Search and Seizure
    (e) Rules of Evidence
    (f) Elements of Laws and Ordinances
    (g) Court room Procedures

(3) Criminal Investigation Techniques
    (a) Receiving and Processing the Complaint
    (b) Elements of Interrogation
    (c) Collection, Identification and Preservation of Evidence
    (d) Scientific Aids of Investigation

    (e) Techniques of Investigating of Specific Offenses
    (f) Fundamentals of the Lie Detector
    (g) Surveillance
    (h) Juvenile Procedures
    (i) Use of Informants
    (j) Criminal Identification
    (k) Procedures in Protecting and Securing Crime Scene

(4) Patrol Techniques
    (a) Principles and Purposes of Patrol
    (b) Techniques and Mechanics of Arrest and Search of Prisoners
    (c) Geography of Area
    (d) Communication and Radio Techniques
    (e) Report Writing
    (f) Description of Persons and Property
    (g) Practical Patrol Practices
    (h) Care and Use of Equipment
    (i) Flash Recognition
    (j) Police Communications
    (k) Handling of Persons

(5) Traffic Control and Traffic Investigations
    (a) Techniques in Traffic Enforcement
    (b) Traffic Engineering
    (c) Mechanics of Traffic Control
    (d) Traffic Accident Investigation
    (e) Accident Investigation Procedure
    (f) Emergency Run Procedures
    (g) Use and Care of Automotive Equipment
    (h) Defensive and Pursuit Driving

(6) Human Behavior
    (a) Dealing with Incompetent Persons
    (b) Dealing ith Minority Groups
    (c) Crowd Control
    (d) Recognizing the Mentally Ill
    (e) Principles of Sociology

(7) Armed and Unarmed Defense
    (a) Firearms Training
    (b) Unarmed Defense — Judo, etc.

(8) Public Relations

    (a) Personal Appearance
    (b) Courtesy and Conduct
    (c) Personal Conduct
    (d) Press Relations
    (e) Telephone Manner
    (f) Basic Importance of Public Relations

In addition to the above, the following subjects should be considered if needed by the group or individuals.

    (a) Spelling
    (b) Effective Speaking
    (c) English
    (d) Driver Training
    (e) Philosophy of Policing and the Police Department
    (f) Typing
    (g) Subversive Activities
    (h) Federal Civil Rights Legislation

In-service Retraining

Even if the recruit training is good, refresher courses are necessary. Probably "Inservice Retraining" is not the proper title for this training as some of the courses in the recruit training program are retraining as are some of the courses in the Supervisors training program and other programs. Here we are referring to the periodic retraining courses for all officers.

It is obvious that such retraining is essential. Procedures change, new laws are passed and old statues are given different interpretations by the courts. The type of courses given in such training depends on many things; (1) The length of time since previous training, (2) the thoroughness of previous training, (3) how well the officers have been advised of changes by the supervisors in daily contacts, (4) the extent departmental procedures have changed, (5) the special problems of the department and many other factors.

Some of the subjects that should be considered in determining the retraining curriculum are listed on the following page.

(1) Administrative Procedures

    (a) Changes in Agency Organization

(b) Review of Procedural Rules and Regulations

(c) Evaluation of the Police Manual (Panel)

(d) Refresher Course in Personnel and Disciplinary Procedures

(e) Evaluation of Departmental Procedures

(f) Crime Prevention on a District Level

(g) Extradition Procedures

(h) Reading for Self-Improvement

(2) Laws and Criminal Procedures

(a) New and Amended Laws and Ordinances

(b) Effect of Court Decisions on Police Procedure

(c) Refresher Course in Liabilities of Police Officers

(d) Review of Local Court Cases with Emphasis on Court room Procedure and Preparation of cases

(3) Criminal Investigation Techniques

(a) Police Interrogation. (Demonstration or panel)

(b) Collection, Identification, and Preservation of Evidence (Review and New Methods)

(c) New Scientific Aids in Investigation. (Demonstration and Discussion)

(d) Causes and Investigation of Crimes of High Incidence

(e) Investigation of Juvenile Offenses

(f) Psychological Aspects of Interrogation

(4) Patrol Techniques

(a) Communication Procedures (Review and Discussion)

(b) Field Reports (Discussion and Critique)

(c) Refresher Course in Patrol Procedures

(d) Evaluation of Patrol Methods (Panel)

(e) Problem Areas in Patrol

(f) Civil Disturbance Control

(5) Traffic Control and Traffic Investigation

(a) Traffic Violator Contacts (Demonstration and Discussion)

(b) Uniformity in Point Control of Traffic

(c) New Techniques in Traffic Investigation

(d) Evaluation of the Traffic Enforcement Program

(6) Human Behavior

(a) Adolescent Problems and Development

  (b) Character Disorders
  (c) Role of the Police in Dealing with Tensions
  (d) Psychology in Policing
(7) Armed and Unarmed Defense
  (a) Firearms Training (Refresher Course)
  (b) Unarmed Defense (Refresher Course and New Techniques)
(8) Public Relations
  (a) Department Evaluation of Public Relations (Panel)
  (b) Public Education as it Relates to Public Relations
  (c) Importance of the Individual to Public Relations
  (d) Ethics and Public Relations

As mentioned, many more suggested courses could be included. These are not to be considered as excluding others. The special needs of the department as determined by records, complaints, and other factors will indicate the courses needed in the inservice retraining program.

Supervisory Training

Until recently, few departments have given training to the supervisors. The change from the worker to the first line supervisor is so great it can not be over emphasized. The supervisor can no longer depend upon his own skills to get the work done but must get results through others. To do this effectively, he needs further training.

Some of the subjects that should be given in the supervisors courses are listed. Again these are not inclusive. Some of these could have been given in other courses. Some others will be necessary to complete the training of men for the supervisor's responsibility. These should be given consideration.

  (1) What the Department Expects from its Supervisors
  (2) The Supervisor's job as compared to the workers
  (3) Leadership on the Job
  (4) Taking Personnel Action
  (5) Handling Behavior Problems
  (6) Starting the New Employee
  (7) Day to Day Job Instruction
  (8) Performance Appraisal and Action following Appraisal

    (9) Establishing and Restudying a Job
  (10) Determining Training Needs
  (11) Effective Use of Time
  (12) Supervisory Reports
  (13) Field Techniques in Supervision
  (14) Administration and Organization of the Department
  (15) Supervisory Planning

Other basic subjects listed under the recruit and inservice retraining courses should be included if necessary.

Training of Specialists

As there are many fields of specialization in the modern police department, it is impossible to include even the basic subjects that should be covered. In many instances, this training can be obtained more economically outside of the department. If, however there are sufficient men in the department who require specialized training, the training officer should consider having the experts in the department give this training with assistance from outside.

Training of Administrators

As indicated at the beginning of this chapter, most of the administrators in the police agencies are selected from the ranks. Unless these top administrators have received administrative training while in the police agency, they probably know only the administrative policies in practice within the department and these through experience. Formal training of administrators is obviously necessary if new techniques in administration are to be acquired and practiced.

Many schools outside of the department are available for those who are or will be police administrators. In many, probably most, departments, the number of police administrators will not justify a training program within the department. If it is determined that administrators will be given formal training within the department, the courses indicated should be considered as basic.

  (1) Principles of Police Administration
  (2) Principles of Police Organization
  (3) Police Management

(4) Police Personnel Management
(5) Coordination with other Agencies
(6) Problems of the Police Administrator
(7) The Police and the Public

Each of the above subjects include many sub topics. These are not broken down as many good books have been written on these topics.* In addition to these specific courses on police administration it should be pointed out that the police administrator should be completely familiar with the laws that determine the authority of the police agency, must have a thorough knowledge of effectively training others and communicating with others, and have an understanding of Human Behavior. If these are not covered elsewhere in the training program, they must be covered here.

Since the administrator will have many duties, many departments are now requiring that the top administrator have college training. This is necessary to give them the broad background necessary to carry out the many and varied functions of the modern police agency.

CLOSING

Summary

In this chapter we have discussed the general and specific objectives of the police training program and have indicated some of the courses that should be considered in the various phases of the training program. For convenience of discussion the training in the police department was broken down into phases. These were: 1) Recruit training program, 2) Inservice retraining program, 3) Supervisory training program, 4) Training of Specialists, and 5) Training of Administrators.

In considering the courses suggested, we again point out that these should not be considered as excluding others, but should be given consideration. Although some states such as New York have

---

* Municipal Police Administration, International City Managers Association, 1313 East 10th Street, Chicago, Ill.; *Police Organization and Management*: V. A. Leonard, Foundation Press; *Police Planning*: O. W. Wilson, Thomas; *Management and Organization*: Allen, McGraw Hill Co.

state agencies which recommend the content of the training programs, training within the departments is not uniform. Some uniformity is desirable but never to the extent that the department will not meet the peculiar needs of that department.

Closing Statement

The departmental training officer, working with the chief, must determine the courses for training within the department. To a very great extent, the success or failure of the agency will be determined by the training program.

INDEX

T.S.